P9-CAO-654

# WINNING THE
# WAR FOR TALENT

RECRUIT, RETAIN, DEVELOP AND WIN

## Chris Czarnik

CAREER [RE]SEARCH GROUP
APPLETON, WISCONSIN

Copyright © 2018 by Chris Czarnik.

All rights reserved. No part of this publication may be reproduced, distributed or transmitted in any form or by any means, including photocopying, recording, or other electronic or mechanical methods, without the prior written permission of the publisher, except in the case of brief quotations embodied in critical reviews and certain other noncommercial uses permitted by copyright law. For permission requests, write to the publisher, addressed "Attention: Permissions Coordinator," at the address below.

Career [RE]Search Group
6 Olde Paltzer Lane
Appleton, WI 54913
www.chrisczarnik.com

Book Layout ©2018 BookDesignTemplates.com


Ordering Information:
Quantity sales. Special discounts are available on quantity purchases by corporations, associations, and others. For details, contact the "Special Sales Department" at the address above.

Winning the War for Talent/Chris Czarnik. —1st ed.
ISBN 978-0-692-13846-5

# Dedication

*No work of this magnitude is achieved alone. Thanks go out to the many people that have been in my life that have contributed their wisdom and experience to this book:*

**Dr. Susan May, president of Fox Valley Technical College who believed in my work before anyone knew I existed.**

*To the best managers that I have ever had in my career. You all showed me what real leadership looks like.*

*Tim Allen*

*Patti Jorgensen*

*Bruce Weiland*

*Bill Guilbeault*

*Roger Johnson*

*To the thousands of job seekers that have trusted me with their search. Your stories are the true authors of this work.*

# Contents

# Contents

# Foreword

## What do you do when the well runs dry?

Imagine for a moment that you have lived in your home for thirty years. You know every nook and cranny of the house. In a pinch, you could make your way through the house during the dark of night (so as not to wake your family). There are virtually no surprises with your house.

Each day for thirty years you have walked up to the sink, turned on the faucet and water runs freely. No matter which faucet you go to in your home, you turn the handle and water pours forth. Sometimes the temperature of the water that is coming out is not quite right for its intended purpose, so you need to adjust the position of the handle to make the water warmer or colder. The amount of water that comes out of the faucet is easily controlled with minimal adjustment and when you don't need water you simply turn the handle to off.

Occasionally you turn the handle and it doesn't work quite right. Maybe the faucet leaks. Sometimes when you turn the handle it comes right off in your hands. Occasionally the lines get plugged and no water comes out. In those cases, you know to call a plumber who has the water flowing again the same day. But mostly the faucet delivers EXACTLY what you want EXACTLY when you need it. When you need water, it is always there in the volume and temperature that you need it. Frankly you long ago stopped thinking about water's availability in your home.

One day you wake up and get ready to take a shower. Barely awake you stumble into the shower and turn on the water the same way you had for thirty years.

**NOTHING COMES OUT OF THE SHOWER HEAD!**

Frustrated, you begin to try everything that has worked for you in the past. You turn the shower handle in both directions-nothing. You pull off the shower head and clean it out because that was the problem five years ago when the same thing happened- nothing. Walking to each of the other faucets in the house you get the same result-nothing. So you call the plumber as you have in the past. He has bailed you out many times before when you had trouble with the water flow in your house.

The plumber does a complete sweep of all of the pipes and valves in the house. All of the things in your house that you have control over are in perfect working order. So you go to your neighbor's house to borrow some water. Surely this is a short term problem and you can just get help from someone in the same situation you are. Same neighborhood, same water supply, same access over the past thirty years. Your neighbors don't have any water either and have no idea what to do.

For the first time ever you have no idea what to do. You start to understand that you have no control over this situation with the tactics that have worked in the past. With a little investigation you realize that the well that the whole city has relied on for those thirty years has dried up. Nobody knows exactly what to do...new thinking isn't a luxury...it is an absolute necessity.

*Water is the lifeblood of a house.*
*Employees are the lifeblood of a business.*

<u>**Welcome to the new age of hiring. That which you have taken for granted is no longer readily available.**</u>

<u>**How you react to it is the difference between life and death for your business.**</u>

## CHAPTER 1

# Where did all the people go and when are they coming back?

The shortage of workers in the United States is being treated like some type of surprise. Anybody paying attention wouldn't be surprised. This shortage has been a mathematical certainty for more than three decades. While there have been fluctuations in employment over that period this "silver tsunami" was always coming. Most companies and organizations didn't plan for this changing demographic because they chose not to look. In many cases the focus on the next quarter's profits overshadowed the looming hiring crisis that has been inevitable since the 1960's.

For businesses to not focus or realize that this was coming is kind of ironic really. With an intense focus on the math of doing business you would have thought that someone would have picked up on this eventuality somewhere along the way.

**The math goes like this...**

## The Baby Boomers

There are somewhere around 74.9 million people in the generation referred to as the baby boomers. That refers to people that were born between 1945 and 1964. Much has been made about the economic impact of this generation as their movement through every phase of life has shaped the economy of this country. Whether it was the sale of diapers (which lead to the creation of disposable diapers, (thank goodness) the proliferation of automobiles (in their teens), the housing boom (as new parents), the unprecedented growth of the workforce (including many women joining the workforce for the first time) and even the explosion of the motor home industry as this giant generation headed towards more leisure activities and retirement.

Businesses closely tracked their movement through their life cycle as they were responsible for most of the profitable trends in the U.S. Life and business was good as long as you were paying attention to this enormous group of people and anticipated their needs. Whole industries were born to service them.

In terms of employees this group created an almost endless supply of labor. For the better part of the last 40 years there was no question about having people available to fill positions. "If you post the job, they will come" was the battle cry of HR managers. The trouble was not many organizations planned on what to do when they moved into retirement and left the market.

## Generation X

The generation that came immediately following the Baby Boomers is referred to as Generation X. This group of people were born between 1965 and 1982.

For many social and economic reasons this generation is a good deal smaller than the Baby Boomers. With approximately 65 million people in Generation X there are fully 10 million less people born during the same number of years that were born during the Baby Boom.

Let's just sit with that for a moment. There are 10 million less people born during that time than the generation immediately preceding it. So as wonderful as it is that the labor market and number of jobs in America expanded dramatically during the Baby Boomer years, the sucking sound that you hear every time that you post a new job today is the vacuum created by 65 million people trying to fill the jobs of 75 million people. See? There is no magic here. No need for a complex explanation about what types of work were glamorized for teen Gen Xers during their youth affecting their career path choices. No need to discuss the push towards 4 year college as the only educational option at the expense of internships in the trades. No need to discuss the comparative work ethic of generations. The fact is that we have 10 million less people to fill the jobs that are being vacated.

See? It was there for everyone to see for 40 years. Let's call it an "inconvenient truth" for people who were so busy making money and growing profit margins to notice. Undeniable, unmistakable, impossible to miss...unless you aren't looking.

## The false hope of the Great Recession

If you do the math with the overlay of one generation and the other you might come up with an interesting question. "Shouldn't this shortage have started to show itself a decade ago?" Why yes...yes it should have.

Except for the one event that could have hidden it from those who were actually looking. The Great Recession.

The math (when these population changes should have started showing up in the labor market) says that we should have begun to see these changes sometime around 2007; 62 years (normal retirement age of the oldest baby boomers) after 1945. People who study demographics were already shouting from the rooftops in the early 2000's that the shortage was coming. Then the most deceptive thing happened.... the world economy fell off a cliff.

The Great Recession artificially decreased the number of jobs needed in America at almost the exact same time the demographers were having U.S. businesses bracing for impact. The shortage never materialized. In fact, due to the massive, temporary decrease in the number of jobs in America, it appeared to business leaders that this shortage was really a hoax that was never going to come to fruition. Many of them decried the warnings that were being sent out as false fear.

Between 2007 and 2012 not only wasn't there a labor shortage, there were many more people looking for work than jobs needing to be filled. Each job opening was met with literally hundreds of applicants. HR managers were blessed with their choice of the best and brightest for each opening. Some less reputable companies actually started treating their existing employees worse or even with contempt as their overconfidence about the labor market grew. Not only did it appear that there was to be no labor shortage but magically there were MORE people available to hire from than ever before. Oh happy day! For five full years there was no urgency because we often look at the next quarter in business instead of looking at the next quarter century.

## Someone needs to pay the Piper

In response to the Great Recession, a college's visionary president hired me to create a program to teach proactive job search to displaced mid-career professionals that were affected by the economic downturn. Over the next ten years I would train more than 2,000 of these people to do a research based job search that I created called "Human Search Engine". During this time I spent every day in the middle of the battle for employment with people who had lost their family sustaining jobs through no fault of their own. My point of view on this time is not theory from the "ivory tower". My job day and night for a decade was to help those who had lost their job and were now in fear of losing their house. Let's just say during that time I became one of the nation's experts on job search even to the point of my process being adopted by the EAP program in Congress.

Somewhere around 2012 a funny thing happened. The number of people that were coming to my classes started to go down. At one point in 2009 I had two full classes of 40 desperate job seekers each hoping for a new opportunity. By 2011 I had to cut the number of classes down to one as there just weren't that many people looking anymore. The number of people coming to the class gradually declined over the next three years.

In 2015 I got the opportunity to become the manager of the Employment Connections department that served our college's graduates in finding employment. By the end of 2015 a shift was absolutely noticeable. No longer were we besieged by job seekers looking for work. Now almost every call that I received was from an EMPLOYER who was having trouble finding people for their jobs! The same employers that would not get back to applicants a year earlier were now literally receiving NO applicants for their job postings.

The shortage of workers that had been predicted for so many years was finally a reality. Most employers had no idea how to react to this because they had never experienced it before. That is the purpose of this book. To bring you new ideas of how to recruit, retain and develop talent in your organization.

Some of these ideas can create a new paradigm for how you deal with your employees. I hope that these ideas create a work environment that not only leads to a self- staffing organization but allows you to grow your employees so that succession planning and filling unexpected openings becomes a non-issue. That is the promise of this book.

For the rest of you, take heart. There are 75.4 million people in the generation that comes after generation X that we call the millennials. That's right....this group of potential workers is actually bigger than the Baby Boomers! The oldest members of this generation are now about 35 years old. That means that you only have about ten years to wait in order for this group to be experienced and mature enough to take over leadership roles in your organization. So you have a choice. Wait ten years trying to run your organization less than fully staffed or implement these ideas to make your organization an employer of choice. If you become the employer of choice in your area or industry you will never need to worry about a shortage of talent. That will be some other company's problem...

CHAPTER 2

# Farmers and Hunters of Talent

If you are struggling finding enough people, or the right people to staff your organization your initial response might be to walk down to your HR area and give them a nudge. Maybe a pep talk will do it. Maybe explaining the effects on customer service that being short staffed is having would work. Some of the worst business managers and owners will pressure their HR staff to "do better whatever it takes". These businesses are going to struggle for the next decade. Why? Because almost everyone in the business world has grown up in a world where finding talent was as easy as posting a job in the newspaper...or more recently on the internet. "If you post it they will come" has been the answer.

When that doesn't work some managers will go immediately to offering more money to attract talent. That lever has worked for them in the past. When that doesn't work most business owners have fired every bullet in their clip and are out of ideas. This leads to additional stated or implied pressure on HR to "step it up or else". The fact is if HR knew what to do they would have done it already. The fact is that these HR people have no more idea of how to find talent than the boss that is pressuring them. What then?

Another important shift in thinking for HR folks is that the people they will be recruiting will not be unemployed...but under-employed. With 3.5% unemployment there just aren't thousands of people sitting at home looking for work. That lake is all but dried up. The real opportunity is to find and recruit people into their next higher level of opportunity in YOUR organization. Hunting for talent will be an absolute requirement for companies that want to grow.

---

### Willing and Able

In every book that I write I capitalize two words every time I use them: WILLING and ABLE. The reason is that I believe that anytime someone does not achieve what you ask of them you have to ask them and yourself if they were UNWILLING or UNABLE to accomplish the task. Let's take a moment to define terms shall we?

*UNABLE- Lacks the physical or mental capacity to achieve the desired outcome. The needed resources may be training, tools or technical knowledge. They want to complete the task but physically cannot without additional resources.*

*UNWILLING- Physically and mentally capable of completing the task but lacks the proper motivation. Push back or lack of understanding of its importance is the limiting factor.*

You may choose to stop at this moment and consider the ramifications of classifying every task that is not completed into one of these two categories. Whether it is a child not cleaning their room or a scientist not curing the common cold this clarification simplifies every issue of this type. The way I see it, anytime someone says they CAN'T do anything (including yourself) figuring out if they were UNWILLING or UNABLE to complete the task is the critical first step. The reason is that once you have this answer you can determine how to proceed. Does the person (again, look in the mirror my friend) lack resources or motivation? This is critical for managers as often times we mistake UNABLE for UNWILLING and think that people are testing our authority. As my good friend and mentor once mused:

"Almost never does someone do something to purposely challenge your authority. It is either that they didn't understand you, don't know how or thought they had a better way. Your job as a manager is to find out which of these is true." Those words have stayed with me for almost 30 years.

With these ideas in mind I would like for you to consider what a lack of employees in your organization really means...both for your HR department and potential employees.

The central question to this entire concept is this:

***Are people UNWILLING or UNABLE to come to work for your organization?***

Think about the ramifications of that question for a moment. In solving your staffing issue, it is imperative that you discover which of these two scenarios are true.

<u>Either:</u>

*People are not coming to work for your organization because they do not know it exists, don't know what your organization does or has no idea there are open opportunities there.*

*People know everything that they need to know about your company and have made a value-based decision not to become part of your organization.*

It is very easy for an organization who is not getting qualified applicants to jump to conclusions about why.

Famously, employers will say things like:

*"Nobody wants to work anymore!"*
*"Those millennials have no work ethic and are living in their parent's basement."*
*"Everybody knows that we are looking but nobody is applying."*

While these statements are certainly popular they are far from true. They really are vague generalities that frustrated HR people use to justify in their own mind that the lack of applicants is "the world's fault" and there is nothing that they can do about it. It's what people say when they don't know what else to do to fix the problem. The real answer however lies in the "Unwilling or Unable" question that I posed earlier. Let's look at both of these and see what's likely going on.

___

## People are UNABLE to work for you because they have never heard of you

By far the number one reason that companies are not receiving applications is that the people looking for jobs have no idea that you have jobs available. There are really two separate problems here:

**1. The people you are trying to reach have no idea that your company exists.**

If you are an HR manager or business owner you are likely completely consumed by your organization. You spend most of your waking moments thinking about your business. That focus is exactly why you might be making the mistake of thinking that people know your business exists. The idea that anyone not knowing that your business exists is an affront to the thousands of hours that you have spent building and growing your organization. Because YOU know it so well...EVERY-ONE must know it that well. That is just not true. My guess is that unless you are an employer of 500 people or more 90% of the people in your geographic area have never heard of your organization. I know, that's hard to hear.

In my small town there are about 80,000 people. Add in the surrounding communities and the population grows to about 250,000. I have lived in this community my entire life (55 years). My work both as a job search expert and as the Career Services manager of the largest technical college in the area would make me one of the areas experts on what companies exist in our region.

If you gave me a pen and paper and 24 hours (and a dollar for each company I named) I could write the names of about 200 businesses in our area without using online resources. That's not too bad until you realize that according to Reference USA there are *34,588* hiring organizations within 30 miles of Appleton.

You see...it's my job to know what's out there and I could name about 1 in 100 of the organizations in my city. If that is true for me, what do you think is true for the average job seeker? If they do not see your company name in the newspaper, in online ads or on a hiring site they very likely have no idea that you exist. And there is no way that they can come to work for your organization unless they know it exists.

Go ahead-test this theory. Walk down the street in your community and randomly ask strangers what they know about your organization. Have they ever heard of it? Do they know what you do? Did they have any idea that you were currently hiring? As importantly, to test the theory go to any online tool that lists companies in your city. Start reading the list. How many of these companies have YOU never heard of?

*That's right, the most likely reason BY FAR that you are not getting applicants is that the outreach efforts to those job seekers is woefully inadequate.*

**2. People are absolutely aware of your organization and they know everything that they need to know about working there. They are making a conscious choice NOT to come to work for you.**

As hard as it is to swallow the fact that people have no idea that your company exists, the realization that some people have evaluated the offering of working at your company and have chosen to work elsewhere should scare you even more. It's not that everyone should want to come to work for you...far from it. Many people will not have the skill set or interest in the work that you do. I'm talking about the people who have learned about your organization and have chosen to walk away.

While it would be easy to be offended by people turning down a job offer from your organization, a great deal can be learned from them by asking their reason for declining your offer of employment. Without asking these questions of them you may automatically think their decision was about the pay or the work was too hard. This would be a normal reaction because it allows you to protect your ego. If your goal is to fill your organization with talent then you desperately need to know why people are walking away.

One last thing on this topic. If you brush off not having enough talented employees on the idea that people just don't want to work anymore, *why are other people choosing to go do the exact same work for your competitors?* Some people are choosing to do the exact same work under very similar circumstances; they just don't want to do it for you. Ouch!

---

## Turning Farmers into Hunters

Examining whether people are UNWILLING or UNABLE to come to work for you is the most important thing that you can do as part of this journey. Without this knowledge you have no idea what to change in order to change your recruiting process. The one thing that is sure is that you need to utilize the two real recruiting tools that you have at your disposal every day. Your HR team and your own employees.

It would not be too much of a stretch to say that the average HR professional knows very little about finding talent in a proactive way. Posting a job ad has always been enough and their biggest concern was how to sort through the piles of resumes that flowed in. With the advent of LinkedIn (which I consider to be the biggest advance in job search in the past 20 years) HR can reach out into the community to make potential employees aware of your hiring opportunities. Actively recruiting talent really comes down to getting out from behind the HR desk and becoming active in the community.

After serving as the career services manager for one of the largest technical colleges in the state of Wisconsin, I can tell you that in my experience HR folks don't do a very good job at all in using educational facilities as recruiting centers. That never made any sense to me as we were training and graduating students that were exactly what they were looking for. Many companies were desperately trying to find and hire welders and electricians. Not many of them chose to visit the campus to set up on campus recruitments or put on student lunches.

In addition to trying to meet students, being part of the advisory board for one of the technical college's departments would provide almost unlimited access to instructors that were working with students every day that companies were trying to find. So why didn't they do it?

My guess is that they did not know what programs the college provided and spent zero time interacting with our career services area to find ways to get in front of our students.

Proactive recruiting at a very base level boils down to identifying the organizations that train people with your desired skill set and working endlessly to create a relationship with them. I would often shake my head as students looking for jobs would ask for help in the morning and the companies looking for those same future employees would call that afternoon.

**If you want to go fishing for trout, first you must find the trout pond.**

In order to be successful implementing proactive recruiting practices for your HR organization you need to turn HR into a sales minded organization. Having a person come to work in your organization is a commitment for both the new employee and the company. It is someone committing their time and effort and part of their life to your organization. They have many choices about where they can go to utilize their talents, so YOU must convince them that choosing your organization is a good life decision for them. I'm guessing that sounds very different from the traditional recruiting efforts that you have done...but how have those been working for you lately?

*But before we go fishing for anything...we better make sure we are using the right bait!*

## Going fishing with the wrong bait

Most baby boomers were taught from a very young age to be driven by security. Baby Boomers (as a whole) were taught that being happy in the job was secondary to being in a job that you can have for the rest of your life. The idea that you actually should be happy in your job would be laughed at by most baby boomers. It would seem like a luxury to them and something that only spoiled children would ask for. Work is pain. The only question is, "how much pain are you willing to put up with for how much money?" That is the equation that defined the baby boomer generation and how they interacted with their job their happiness and their money.

Remember that most of the baby boomer generation learned how to live from people who went through the Great Depression. And even though the baby boomer generation as a whole was not part of that Great Depression, their parents were. And so the way that they created their attitude around money, savings, security, work and family were formed for the most part simply out of the emotion of fear. Their parents lived in a world where not only wasn't there any money but everything was rationed. Security was the only thing that mattered because there was so little of it going around. If you are a baby boomer hiring manager, take a look back at the messages that you received as you were growing up about work and you will notice that many of them surrounded the idea that having a job, any job was a luxury and not something to be taken for granted. That having a job, any job, was better than being out on the street trying to sell apples for a nickel to feed your family. The lessons of the Great Depression (which now is some 80 + years ago) are still forming the opinions of the people currently trying to **recruit** this new generation. While the lessons of the Great Depression including savings and responsibility are very positive ideas, it is clear that to make all of your decisions based on fear in today's age is a mistake. And more importantly the millennial worker will not react to that messaging and will fact will run screaming in the opposite direction.

---

## Start with a Different Mindset

The first important thing to understand about Millennials is that they are not generally motivated by security. The problem with this of course is that we are trying to use the values of the baby boomer generation to motivate millennial workers.... and there's the rub.

What is important to understand is that the millennial generation was the first generation to grow up with access to the internet. What this means is that they had the sum total of all the knowledge of the history of the world available to them within 10 or 15 seconds simply by typing a few words into Google. Why is that so important when we discuss how to motivate Millennials in a work setting? Well for most of us the idea of struggling to find out information or the idea of looking for something new was pretty tedious. If you really wanted to look for a new job as a baby boomer you spent days with the newspaper or at the library. That kind of research made most of us decide that was too much work and we would simply stay in the job that was making us unhappy... but was paying the bills.

Nothing could be further from the truth for the millennial generation. From their very first days of kindergarten if they had a question or were looking for a different option that information was at most 20 or 30 seconds away. Advice, guidance feedback options were as much a part of their day as was the Baby Boomer's alarm clock going off and going to this job that made their stomach churn.

This easy access to information, options and problem solving is something that the baby boomer generation did not grow up with. This however creates the tension and the problems when it comes to motivating millennials. *A startling statistic is that the average Millennial in their lifetime will **change companies**, not jobs but companies every 3 years.* Why? Because they can. Their ability to identify new options, different companies, different organizations, different job types, different levels and different responsibilities is as easy for them as ordering a pizza online. This creates a significant issue for the baby boomer manager trying to recruit and retain Millennials.

What is interesting here is that the baby boomer manager might be frustrated by the ability for the millennial worker to have so many options and so much flexibility. Not because they think it's wrong but because there's actual jealousy that they wish they had had access to that many options during their own career. Managers from a different generation may very well see this WILLINGNESS to move from employer to employer and UNWILLINGNESS to put up with any disappointment hardship or frustration in a job as the actions of a spoiled generation. The odd thing of course is that that manager would crave that same flexibility and those same options in their own life but was raised in a different way. In order for HR managers and hiring managers to understand and really connect with millennial employees they first have to get over their own disappointment that the flexibility and options that current workers have are ones that never were available to them. Believe it or not this is one of the major factors in why organizations have struggled so much with connecting and retaining millennial employees.

It does not escape me though that it might occur to a baby boomer manager that this moving from job to job may not serve the millennial worker very well in the future. Much as a parent would, the manager might want to tell the millennial that their moving from job to job and company from company does not set them up to have a stable retirement. The more you look at the frustrations with Millennials the more you will likely see that the frustration comes not from their inability to work or their inability to stay with an organization but more so that they have more options, more possibilities and more flexibility than any other generation in the past. How that will affect them in the future is hard to tell... but it is not our job to guide them to do things that will help them 20 years from now unless they ask us... And most are not asking.

So what does that mean? Relating to the millennial generation starts and ends with their desire for freedom and flexibility; with much less focus on security. Everything we do in this idea of Winning the War for Talent is going to focus on appealing to millennial workers (and even the generations after them with the idea that freedom, flexibility, education and growth will be cornerstones of their career regardless of where they choose to go to work). That also means that the organization has to realize that it no longer gets to set all of the rules around its interaction with employees. The last 30 years have been the easiest hiring generation perhaps in the history of the United States. That means that HR staff and hiring managers have had an overabundance of applicants for every job that they had available. It became so common to have ten qualified people for every job that frankly most of these people forgot about the idea of actually going out and finding talent. In order to succeed in this "new normal" it is now the companies that have to adjust...not the employees.

If you're a manager or owner reading this right now, what I just said might seem upside down. If you are thinking to yourself "This is my organization. I, and only I, will determine what new hires get and what is available to them" you are likely going to the fail over the next 10 years to attract and more importantly retain the talent you need. What you as a hiring executive need to understand is that whether you like the attitude of the millennial generation or not they are the only pool of workers that are available today. The rules have fundamentally changed. It's not so much that the employees are now getting to tell companies what they will and won't do but that there has to be a meeting in the middle ground where a balance between work and home life is a real consideration and not simply something that people talk about in books. Where a balance between work and a family life becomes the norm. Where others lament the fact that they work for organizations that couldn't care less about anything other than producing for the company.

It is absolutely clear that if you are going to stick to your guns and not adapt you will be one of those losers in the war for talent... But it doesn't have to be that way.

It is time for us to embrace what the Millennials already know. That in this new technology age opportunity and possibility is everywhere. The idea of working for one company for 20 or 30 years is a quaint idea. In fact the new reality, the new norm is that *we are all free agents all the time.* You work today, you get paid today, and for the most part that is the extent of the relationship between a company and its workers. You don't believe that's true? The vast majority of states in the United States have what is referred to as "at will" employment law. At-will employment very literally means that the worker could quit at any time for any reason and the company can discharge an employee for virtually any reason outside of those very specifically protected by law.

Trying to sell security as a way to recruit, retain and develop this new generation of workers is like going fishing with bird seed....you're done before you start.

CHAPTER 3

# Steps to Creating a Sales Minded HR Department for your Organization

Imagine for a minute that your sales manager came to you and had a very perplexed look on his face. He is clearly distraught and frustrated. You ask him what's wrong.

"Well, we have tried absolutely everything and we can't find any new customers. Everything we have tried so far has failed. I just think that nobody needs our product anymore and we may really be in deep trouble. I know it's my job to find new customers but it just isn't going anywhere." You might do what any good business owner would do and start asking questions to try to determine the cause of this problem. "What have you tried so far?" you ask.

"We have tried EVERYTHING!" he says. "We put the best marketing minds in the company together and came up with a really great marketing piece for our products and services. We were just so sure that people would respond to it." You ask the next logical question. "So where did you post the marketing piece?"

"Well, we found a huge internet site that gets lots of people looking at it every day and we put it up on there. Thousands of people go to that site every day and so we just kind of waited for the phone to start ringing and the orders to start pouring in."

You are incredulous. "Did you go out and prospect for any customers face to face?" No. "Did you contact our current customers to get referrals from them for new customers?

No. "Did you create a profile of our existing customers and use research tools to identify other companies that might need our products and services?" No. You are beyond frustrated with the short sightedness of your sales manager. They posted an ad and just waited for customers to walk through the door? That's crazy!

*Now, if you wouldn't accept that level of effort from your sales team why are you accepting that level of effort from your HR team that is looking for new employees?*

The search for new employees can utilize many of the same prospecting ideas that salespeople use to find customers. But it requires proactive thinking and a WILLINGNESS to get out from behind the desk for the HR staff.

## What steps to take to create a sales focused HR group

There are several things that you need to do to prepare your HR team to go and actively seek talent. These steps will look familiar to you as they will very likely mimic the way that you have done sales for your company's products and services. Sales is sales regardless of what you are selling. Going through this process will help you learn a great deal about your organization.

---

## 1. Create messaging

Regardless of what your company sells or provides you probably have spent a great deal of time coming up with messaging about your product or service to make it appeal to your customer. I'd like for you to begin thinking about selling your organization as a place to work in the same way.

It is helpful for you to consider some questions while creating this messaging:

*Who am I selling to? What is the profile of the type of person that I am hoping will join our organization?*

*What is their background?*

*What education or experience do they have?*

*What job did they hold immediately before coming to work for us?*

*What are their goals for employment?*

*What problem does this job solve for an employee?*

*What advantages does this job have over its competitors?*

*Are the benefits financial? Family life? Flexibility? Advancement? Prestige?*

*Who am I selling against and what is my competitive advantage over them?*

*Why are people choosing to go to work for my competitors instead of me?*

## 2. Identify your target customer (employee)

No matter how good your messaging is, if you don't have a good idea of who you are trying to recruit into your organization all of that work will be wasted. No matter how good your messaging is to sell a minivan if you put that message in front of someone looking for a sports car they will be unmoved. Creating a profile of your next great employee is work that you need to do.

This profile will need to include:

*What education does the person have?*

*What experience does the person have?*

*What is the life situation that person has (first job, transitional job, second career, just a job to feed the family)*

*What hobbies or recreational activities does this type of person enjoy? (Birds of a feather flock together)*

*Where does this type of person vacation?*

*What volunteer organizations does this type of person join?*

## 3. Create "models" for the best people in every type of job in your organization

It is important at this point to see that we use this type of "modeling" in our own lives every day. If we want to lose weight we befriend people who live a healthy lifestyle to learn from them. If we want to be successful in business we get the advice, guidance and feedback of people who have had successful business careers. Young people very often seek the advice of people with more life experience than them to make sure that they do not recreate the mistakes of the past.

Something that seems to always be true is that people hang out with people that are like themselves. In high school I don't remember any of my debate friends hanging out with the cheerleaders. The athletes didn't spend a lot of time with the "mathletes".

While we will make huge generalizations inside this model, our goal is to identify people similar to your best employees and put our marketing materials in front of them. This can be easily done through a process of internal interviewing of your best employees in each area of your organization. The process might look something like this:

Identify the general traits that make employees a great fit for YOUR organization. This might include their abilities to communicate, show creativity, have initiative, solve problems, or being a great team player or leader. This positive profile will be used as an overarching guideline for all of your hiring.

Create categories of jobs inside your organization. This will most likely revolve around the skill set and personality type of your best people in that area of your organization.

Interview your best people in each area of your organization to identify the answers to these questions (see #2 in this chapter). These people MUST volunteer for this interview and you need to be clear with them about why you are gathering this information. When you explain to them that you are looking to fill their department with more people like them they are usually quite honored to be interviewed.

# 4. Creating "career quadrants" to categorize jobs inside your organization into 4 categories

For most organizations if we tried to create a profile for every job inside the organization it would take us the better part of a year. Many organizations have dozens of job titles all with differing duties and responsibilities. This would be a Herculean task and would be too complex and take too much time for most companies. The idea of assigning each job inside your organization into a "career quadrant" will allow you to create profiles for only four types of employees.

**The four quadrants are:**

Work primarily with people - Works with people to improve or modify their effectiveness individually or as part of a team. (Counselor, HR)

Work primarily with process - Works to create a process where a series of actions create a predictable result that is reliable and repeatable. (Example: Accountant/Engineer)

Communicate with people primarily in person - Primary and most comfortable interacting with people face to face. Good at reading social cues and adapting to the person.

Communicate with people primarily through technology - Communication is more impersonal and systematic. Accuracy of information is most important...not connection with the person. (E-mail/phone)

|  | People | Process |
|---|---|---|
| **In Person** |  |  |
| **Through Technology** |  |  |

In this exercise you will choose one from #1 and #2. Then you will choose one from #3 and #4. The four types of job descriptions would be:

*Works primarily with people and communicates through technology (Customer service person)*

*Works primarily with people and communicates with people in person (shift supervisor or team lead)*

*Works primarily with process and communicates with people in person (maintenance technician)*

*Works primarily with process and communicates through technology (IT support person)*

Now go through each job category in the organization and classify it under one of these four categories. After that is completed, find a great employee in each of the four categories and create the aforementioned model of them. With these four completed profiles you now have the ability to recruit people who will naturally fit into these types of jobs.

## Where are you advertising your opportunities and who is actually seeing them?

Why do thousands of organizations use websites like Monster and Indeed to advertise their job openings? They are low or no cost options. They are widely known by job seekers. They are well known in the business community. They have quality control and even have matching systems available. They are easy and require almost no work or commitment. Seems like the perfect way to advertise your job right?

### So why isn't it working for you?

Steven Covey was a brilliant man. He wrote several books during his lifetime; the most popular by far being "Seven Habits of Highly Effective People". This book sold millions of copies and is still used to guide people's lives and their businesses to this day. It is in my opinion one of the truly life changing self-help books ever written. If you haven't read it...I highly recommend it.

One of the concepts that he spends time on in this work was the idea that you have to evaluate any proposed solution to a problem on two axis: *Efficient and Effective.*

> *Efficient means that the solution requires the least time and effort and potentially reaches the most people.*
>
> *Effective means that the solution produces the intended and desired result.*

There are not that many solutions out there for any problem where you can maximize both of these axis. Generally you need to make a choice between varying degrees of both. A very efficient solution might not be very effective. An effective solution might not be very efficient. There are almost always tradeoffs and choices to be made between the two.

Monster and Indeed are highly efficient solutions. Very little work and very little cost. But why are they not bringing qualified candidates to your door? My guess is that many HR people use these because they can tout their efficiency to their boss. Other HR people use it because they have no idea what else to do.

The solutions that I am proposing in this book are for the most part more work and require spending more time and money. *My guess though is that you are reading this book because the highly efficient way of finding good candidates is not working very well for you.* With that in mind let's talk about how to implement targeted and highly effective solutions when you are getting virtually no response from your online job postings.

Modeling gives us clues about not only what to say in the advertisement but also where to focus your marketing time and money.

Let's take for example a roofing company that is having trouble finding qualified people for their roofing technician positions. These entry level positions are very hands on and labor intensive. Some would argue that "nobody wants to do this type of work anymore". Is that true? If it were then why do their competitors have roofing technicians on their payroll? If truly nobody wanted this type of work then EVERY roofing company would have exactly zero people in these roles currently. Clearly that is not the case.

*So who DOES want this type of work?*

## Modeling to the Rescue!

This is where modeling comes in. If a company were to interview their best roofing technicians what would they learn about that employee's path to your company?

*What education or experience did they have?*

*What job did they have immediately preceding coming to work for your roofing company?*

*How do they spend their free time?*

*What else do they use their mechanical aptitude for in their spare time?*

*What hobbies do they have?*

*What classes did they enjoy in high school?*

With this information we can take our marketing documents and make them speak to people who are in the same situation but are not yet in the roofing industry. We can then deploy these marketing pieces in the locations where people with the same interests might spend their time.

Let's say that in conversations with our very best roofing technicians we discover these facts about them:

Most of them took a shop or mechanical class sometime during high school.

They are often involved in home repair for friends and family.

Their favorite place to volunteer their time is Habitat for Humanity.

Their free time on the weekends is often spent working on anything with an engine.

They thought that regular classroom learning in a high school setting was boring and excelled in classes where they could use their creativity and there was a tangible result of their work.

What would you do with this information? What types of organizations would you hope to create relationships with? How would you change your interactions with your local high school or technical college? Would you be more likely to support and sponsor efforts for Habitat for Humanity?

---

## Does this sound like a lot of work? Well what's the alternative?

There is an old saying that goes: *"If you need it bad, you will get it bad"*. Companies pressed for employees need them bad...so they get them bad. Bad fits, bad skills, bad behavior. Companies need qualified people for their organization. They say that their people are their greatest asset. They say they will do ANYTHING to recruit great people into their organization. *Well, we'll see...*

CHAPTER 4

# Why aren't your current employees recruiting for your organization?

It seems to make sense that the fastest, cheapest and easiest way for you to recruit new employees into your organization would be to encourage your current employees to recruit people they know into your organization. This type of referral solves multiple problems for an organization:

*Little work, cost or time spent by HR*

*You get a referral from someone who knows this person well and can vouch for them as an employee*

*The current employee that is referring this person to you has a vested interest (their job!) in making sure that they only refer great people to you who they know will succeed*

*The current employee can explain the job and the organization to the recruit so that they know what they are getting into and come to you with their eyes open.*

This is an almost ideal situation for an employer. So why aren't your current employees referring people into your organization? Chances are that they know people with the same interests and backgrounds that make them a great fit for you. There must be some reason that your employees are not referring people to you. In fact, there are only two:

They are either UNWILLING or UNABLE to refer people that they know to your organization. Doing some research to determine which of these it is can unlock a stream of talented people for you. Let's look at each of these to see what might be going on.

---

## UNABLE

*If your employees do not know that you are looking for employees how can they possibly help you?*

*If they do not know the types of jobs that you are looking to fill how can they refer people?*

*If your employees do not know the type of person that you are looking for in each of the open positions how can they help you?*

*If your employees do not have a clear and easy path to make a referral into your organization how can they help you?*

Each of these scenarios plays out in hundreds of organizations every day. In these organizations there is often a mistaken idea that "everyone knows that we are looking for people". They think this even though they do not have a focused program to explain and promote the idea of referrals into the organization. This is happening more today than ever because even the current employees still believe that there are 10 great applicants for every position that you advertise...because that's the way it has been for the past 25 years.

## Fixing UNABLE

What would a focused program look like for an organization that wants to put some time and effort into it? This could just be a problem of misconception that is playing out both in the minds of the employees and in the minds of HR folks.

Employees might think: "If they wanted me to recruit my friends then they would make a big deal out of it. At the very least they would let me know the types of people that they are looking for and what jobs are open."

At the exact same moment HR people might be thinking: "EVERYBODY knows how hard it is to find people today.

They MUST know that we are not getting many applicants because we are always running short and on overtime." Isn't another possibility that employees think that the short staffing and overtime are just business strategies that are being purposely used?

The first step in remedying this problem is clear communication about the current needs and desires of the business. Never assume that someone working "on the floor" of your company knows what is going on in the minds of the people who are in charge of managing it. As a "floor" employee for almost 10 years myself in three different manufacturing settings I can say with experience that this is almost always a communication problem. Floor employees come in and do their job with great skill and expertise. They do not think recruiting for the company is their concern unless that is clearly and repeatedly stated.

More importantly here is what I learned as a shift supervisor and operations manager. *The people on the floor most likely already have an answer to your problem.* These folks know exactly why people aren't coming to work for your organization. They know if it is a pay or schedule or working conditions problem. They have discussed it dozens of times on their lunch breaks and when they hang out on the weekends. They just aren't telling you.

WHY? Most likely because you haven't asked.

---

## UNWILLING

If your employees really are ABLE to refer people to your organization (know there is a need, know people who might fit and know exactly how to refer them) then you have a larger and more complex problem in your business. It can still be fixed with a dedicated plan but before you can plan anything there is something that you are required to do and it might be painful: ***Find out why people don't want to come to work for you.***

If your employees are UNWILLING to refer their friends to you it is likely because there is something about your organization that they see as a significant negative. No matter how much money you offer them you will never get people to lead their friends into a situation that is perceived as negative. Often companies will up their referral bonus and offer bigger rewards as an effort to increase referrals. That type of action ignores the core question: "What reputation does my company have in the workforce community that makes people go elsewhere?"

Every one of your competitors has employees that have similar skill sets, experience and abilities to the ones you desire in your employees. That means there are two things that are true:

There are people out there who want to do the type of work that you have available

Those people chose to do that work for someone else instead of doing it for you. Why?

### Fixing UNWILLING

If you think about it, if you had the best job in the best organization with the most opportunities to grow (and people knew about it) people would be lined up outside your door to apply. As I have often said, Brad Pitt and Angelina Jolie don't need to take out a billboard ad to get a date. They are perceived by many as beautiful and successful people; a single word about their availability would have people lining up for the chance to meet them. So what is it about your organization that keeps it from being perceived as a great place to work? Let's break it down into four categories.

**Reputation**
**Pay**
**Opportunity**
**Flexibility**

## Reputation

Do you know what your reputation as an employer is? If you think you know, how do you know? I believe that the only way to find out what your reputation in the hiring community is to talk with people that USED to work for you but have move on to somewhere else. Talking to people who currently work for you is not a reliable source of information. Current employees have a tendency to protect their job by saying only positive things when asked.

*Asking a current employee how they rate you as an employer is like asking a beauty pageant contestant if they like the way the pageant is being run.* You will likely only get answers that are candy coated truth.

On the other hand, talking with FORMER employees is a great way to get honest feedback. You may hear things that are hard to hear but that is exactly the feedback that you need. You don't have to choose to interview employees that were disgruntled when they left. You would likely get feedback that is skewed too far negative. The best type of former employee to interview is one that moved into a different industry or moved up to a higher position with another company.

If you do not have a good idea of what your reputation as an employer in your community is you can spend all of the marketing dollars that you want doing recruitment and you will struggle. Worse yet, you will not find out why people are not coming to your organization and falsely assume that "there is no talent out there."

## Pay

I listed pay second here purposely. Many organizations believe that the reason that they are not getting new employees is that they are not the highest paying employer in their industry. This vague, overarching and mostly false assumption keeps many organizations short staffed.

Study after study says that after a certain point of income that allows an employee to create a basic life for themselves (housing, food, transportation and some recreation) that pay quickly drops as an employee's reasons to accept a job or move to a new one. As a matter of fact pay is likely either three or four in this list. So why do so many employers default to this explanation of why people aren't coming? Several reasons really:

*It is the easiest thing to adjust and the easiest thing to blame it on (while not usually true).*

*It is the easiest and least complicated thing to compare yourself against with other employers.*

*If the business is not WILLING to raise its wages then the managers can blame the shortfall on greedy unrealistic employees that don't understand the dynamics of business finances.*

*It is a simple explanation that makes the problem "the world's fault that we can do nothing about."*

*It does not require any in depth research about your organization and keeps you from the pain of discovering what is really going on.*

The easiest way in my opinion to solve the pay issue is to make sure that your entry level wage is at least on par with everyone else. Recruiting young people into your organization means that you will be talking to folks with little work experience and may focus solely on pay to make their decision. This pay gap makes much LESS difference as people move up in the organization. Again, once a person makes enough to meet their basic needs the rest of their needs can be filled with recognition and opportunity.

The biggest danger by far of deciding that pay is the only reason people aren't coming into your organization is that it will keep you from doing the more in depth research that will allow employees not only to choose you. But to stay with you long term.

**Last note:** If you truly are far behind the pay curve compared to other similar employers in your area you HAVE to have something else to sell. Whether it is flexibility, vacation, opportunity or development opportunities, you need a flag to fly to balance the scales. If you are the lowest paying employer in your industry and area and have nothing else that you offer your employees the free market will keep you short staffed.

*Remember, if they come to you for pay....they will leave you for pay.*

---

## Opportunity

When most people start a new job they are not really thinking about tomorrow...they are focused on today. What effect will taking this job have on my family? Will this schedule allow me to spend time with my children? Is this the type of work I want to do and the culture that I want to do it in? What will my day look like? What is expected of me? These are the thoughts going through a job seeker's mind at hire.

The trouble is that for most similar companies the answer to these questions will be roughly the same for an employee whether they come to work for you or your competitor. Opportunity to grow tips the scales in your favor when both opportunities look the same. The opportunity to grow as a person and as an employee creates a future image in the potential employee's mind that has them choosing you. To see themselves as a better person with more options in the future. This is an intriguing image that they can talk about with their spouse or family when they are trying to decide which company to come to work for. Win over the family and friends and you will win over the employee. Painting a mental picture of their future with the company is crucial.

## Flexibility

With people under 35 years old today, flexibility might be the most important category of all. It is also the most overlooked category by most owners and managers.

Why is it overlooked? Well first of all, the people old enough to be running organizations grew up in a different time. People born in the 60's and 70's were mainly taught that the most important trait of any employment was security. Regardless of whether the job fit their personality or skill set, if it was a sure thing they were golden. Happiness in your job was not an expectation for many people in this generation. You would often hear people of this age group say things like, "You are just lucky to have a job...any job!"

Well, things are different when it comes to the expectations of younger workers. Where the older folks valued security, this younger generation values freedom and flexibility. This is a generation that is defined by endless possibilities and instant access to information through the internet. The overwhelming sentiment of this generation is that they would rather be unemployed than be unhappy.

Remember: *The average millennial will change companies every three years during their working life.*

This is disastrous news for organizations that hire and train new employees just to see them walk out the door a few years later. We may not fully understand this shift in priorities and may even wonder how these younger people make their life work with these priorities. Regardless of whether we agree with their thinking or not these are the employees that are out there for us to hire. There are no alternative lakes to go fishing in. We have to go to the fish...the fish no longer have to go to us.

Flexibility can take many forms. Non Traditional work schedules, job sharing, working from home and extended unpaid leaves are tools that you have available to you to speak to this group. Sounds like it might be time to survey some of these folks in your organization to see what types of flexibility might be of benefit to them. Of course you still need to run your business and not everybody gets what they want. But flexibility is often a FREE benefit that is super meaningful to this age group...as well as older employees. Have you ever heard an employee complain about having TOO MUCH flexibility in their work?

## How to Create a Self-Staffing Organization

With what we have just covered it is easy to see why simply offering money to employees to recruit people into your organization doesn't work very well. In addition, if we move through the process of offering only money for a referral it looks like this from the current employee's perspective:

Current employee makes a referral of a new employee.

They are told that if the person is hired and if that person lasts 6 months with the organization they will receive a $500 bonus.

The person is hired and the employee receives NO immediate benefit for putting their personal and professional reputation on the line to benefit the company.

The employee sweats out 180 days of probation for the new hire knowing that if that person does not work out they get nothing.

If the employee makes it through the probation period the employee receives his/her bonus on their next check.

Because the hire is so long ago no one makes any fuss over the success of the hire or thanks the employee that made the referral.

The employee receives a check with the bonus. After taxes the actual amount received is about $325.00.

With that money the employee likely pays a couple of extra bills but there is no lasting emotion about the event.

Next time around the employee decides not to refer another person as the reward for doing so is long in coming, at risk for 6 months and delivered in an unceremonious and silent way with virtually no verbal recognition inside the organization.

After you look at it this way, is it any wonder why your pay for referral program has not worked for you? We need to look at what truly motivates employees and discover what would be enough for the employee to take such a risk.

---

## Every Sale is an Emotional Sale

What the "money for referral" program misses is that money is rarely enough of a motivator for employees to take this leap. Due to the transactional nature and temporary perceived benefit the bonus program is not inspiring to employees at all. They already have some money...so more money is nice but not motivating. What truly motivates people to act is two things:

*Recognition*
*Paid time away from the job*

Why do those two things "move the needle" for employees? Because they both create an emotional attachment to the event. Attaching emotion to an event creates memories, fond feelings that can be relived and permanence for the event. In my work with more than 2,000 individual job seekers I have found one thing to be universally true. True change and learning only happen when the student attaches some emotion to the learning. Let me show you this in your own life.

Do you remember where you were on Sept. 11th, 2001? Yes, that tragic day when terrorists rammed two planes into the World Trade Center, the Pentagon and one that was headed for the White House before it was heroically diverted by the brave, selfless passengers of that flight. Close your eyes for a moment and try to remember the details of how you experienced that day.

*Where were you?*
*What emotion came over you when the news reported the first plane hitting the building?*
*What realization of horror did you experience when the second plane hit the other tower?*
*Who were you with? Who did you call? What conversations did you have?*
*Do you remember that fear in the pit of your stomach even though the event was perhaps hundreds of miles away?*
*What feelings come over you now when you close your eyes and remember that day? Chilling isn't it?*

Now, where were you and what were you doing two days later? Almost impossible to remember right? Those days are almost exactly the same number of years ago and yet one day you can remember in great detail whereas the other day you would be hard pressed to remember even one detail.

The difference between your memories of those two days is based on the fact that the first day had a great deal of emotion attached to it while the second one was quite unremarkable and no strong memory or emotion is attached to it. The same exercise can be done with your wedding day or the birth of your first child. Any day that has deep emotion attached to it is burned into our memory.

What this means is that if we do not create a positive emotion or memory with the referral of a candidate to your company (by an existing employee) the program is doomed to failure. If we utilize the concepts of Recognition and Paid Time Away from their job and create events that generate a positive emotional response, employees will be much more likely to engage with you. Here's how we can do it using both of these concepts:

---

## Recognition

In order to motivate employees to START the process of referring potential employees there needs to be some almost immediate recognition for doing so. In this case the recognition does not need to be in the form of a gift or money. A much more effective way would be an award and open communication of the event to the whole organization.

What you are likely missing here is that referring an employee for hire is loaded with great risk and relatively little reward for your current employees. If the referred person doesn't make it through the hiring process they get nothing...except some good natured kidding from others about their "poor judgement of people". If the referred person doesn't make it through the probationary period it is a constant reminder that your employee took a risk, allowed YOU to evaluate the person through the interview and hiring process and when the company hires them and they don't work out the only one that loses is the referring employee.

Sounds a lot like all risk and very little reward. Still wondering why your "pay for referrals" program isn't producing results?

Recognition for making a referral needs to be immediate and positive for the current employee. This recognition can be as simple as a thank you card with a $20 restaurant card inside it. What if the referral doesn't work out? WHO CARES? How many $20 gift cards would you be willing to give out in order to get one great new employee? Sure there will be some gift cards that don't create a great result but the initial effect is that it gets people talking about the program.

As importantly, the restaurant that you give the gift card to should be a place where an employee would likely take their spouse or significant other. If their spouse has a great night out alone with their partner don't you think that partner will highly encourage the employee to make more referrals?

It is important for you to see here that employees will not generally make referrals for the good of the company. They will make the referral if it benefits them in a way that is immediate, tangible and creates a positive emotional experience. A person's significant other has much more influence over the actions of your employees than you could ever hope to. I believe that the secret to getting referrals flowing in the door is to involve the spouse and make sure that the spouse benefits from the reward for the referral directly.

**In this way the employee receives recognition not only at work, but in the home as well.**

Implement this recognition system in any way that is consistent with your company culture. The key however is to make the recognition public, immediate, positive and involve a significant other if possible.

## Supercharging your Referral program

It is important to create a referral incentive program that truly motivates employees. With money all but off the board (we have discussed its shortcomings as an incentive) the most motivating incentive of all is paid time away from work. You have an opportunity here to create an incentive system that will truly have your employees talking to their friends and neighbors about coming to work for you.

This incentive program would have five main attributes:

- *The incentive is given to the employee when the person that they referred is hired...not after 6 months or a year.*

- *The paid time off is strongly encouraged to be a vacation for the entire family (or at least including the spouse or significant other).*

- *The employee is encouraged to take pictures and use social media to document their time away.*

- *Consent to use those pictures and social media as an advertising tool for the organization would be accompanied by some amount of money that could be used during the trip.*

- *Notices about the availability of this new incentive program needs to be communicated as much as possible to the employees entire household (mass mailing to "the family of" all employees).*

What we know so far in our research is that in order for incentives to work they need to be immediate, significant, create an emotion. The last part of this program is the purposeful communication to the employees' household.

Why?

Picture this conversation at the home of your employee:

*Spouse:* "Honey, we got a letter from your work today that was addressed to the whole family. I opened it and you'll never believe the new program they've started. If you successfully refer someone to work there, you get an EXTRA week of vacation! Even more, they are offering $XXX for us to use on that vacation!

*Employee:* "Yeah, we were told about that a week or so ago. Sounds like a hassle though. We have to introduce someone we know to the company as a potential employee and we only get the extra week of vacation if the company actually hires them."

*Spouse:* "You mean we don't have to wait six months or a year to see if that person works out?"

*Employee:* "No, the company is taking that responsibility on the interview process. I think it makes them want to sharpen their interviewing process and only hire people they really believe that will work out. I can't really think of anyone right now that I would refer so I don't think this applies to us."

*Spouse:* "Are you kidding me? We can finally take the kids to see Mount Rushmore and the Badlands like we have been talking about for years! You only have two weeks of vacation now and that always gets used up for your fishing trip and going to see my parents.

We could have a real family vacation and even have a little money to take up some of the expenses. WE ARE GOING TO FIND SOMEONE TO REFER INTO YOUR COMPANY!"

*Employee:* So I don't know anyone who is looking for a job right now...do you?

*Spouse:* "Let's send an email to all of our friends and ask them if they know any great people that are currently looking for work. Also, we can make it known at church and at my volunteer organization. Don't worry, we will do a thorough screening of anyone that we refer before we recommend them."

*Employee:* "As long as this is important to you and you are WILLING to help me find someone I'm in. I've always wanted to see Mount Rushmore anyway..."

And so it would go. There is little people value more than paid time away from their job to spend with family and friends (once their basic needs are met by working for you). There is a true emotional connection to time away and the memories that are created during that time. Remember, there is NOTHING you can do as an employer to persuade an employee to do something that is one tenth as effective as what that person's significant other can do. Involving the family in this opportunity in any way that you can is the key to the success of this program.

## Creating the force multiplier effect

Once the first person refers someone into your organization successfully and takes the trip that the extra week of vacation provides it is important to use that experience to influence other employees to do the same thing. The goal here is to have the family on their earned vacation document their trip through pictures and social media. The money that you offer them to go on the trip with ($300-$500) would include the companies' access to some of those pictures and social media posts to be used inside the organization. The employee would of course get to decide what you are allowed to use or if they want to exchange access to those pictures at all.

Once you are granted access to those pictures it is time to use them in a multimedia display inside your organization to show other employees what they could have if they refer someone into the organization. You could even send a flyer to each employee's home to celebrate the earned vacation and show others how they could get one as well. Again, making the family aware of the opportunity and creating an EMOTION in their minds to associate with that referral is the key to getting support at home for the employee making a referral.

Remember: people are either UNWILLING or UNABLE to refer people into your organization. It is very important for you to find out which is true (or maybe both are true).

Stop trying to get referrals with money. It may be an efficient way to do it, but has it been EFFECTIVE so far?

---

## Paid Time Away from the Job

### Salaried Employees

First of all I would like to encourage each person reading this book who has employees to consider something about salaried employees:

**I believe that for the most part paid vacation is a ZERO cost benefit for salaried employees.**

Now I can already hear the HR people and the finance people reading this up in arms and disagreeing with that statement. They might argue that there is a real cost to paid time off and that giving extra weeks of vacation to salaried employees drives up the overall cost of pay and benefits for the organization. They might believe that giving this extra week or two of vacation to their salaried employees is a cost without benefit. *I couldn't disagree more.* To prove this let me ask one simple question to see if this is true or not in your organization:

*Do you hire another person to fill that slot when your salaried employees are off on vacation? Does someone literally come into the organization that wasn't there the day before that person went on vacation? Did you pay another employee overtime to cover the duties and responsibilities of the person who is off on paid vacation? If the answer is no then I would argue that vacation is a no cost benefit for your employees and can be used as a benefit to attract talent instead of increasing wages.*

Let's walk through this idea for a moment. What actual increased costs in pay or benefits do you incur when a salaried employee takes vacation? My guess is the answer is ZERO. The reason for this is that one of two things has a tendency to happen when someone in the office goes on vacation:

*Another employee or employees cover a portion of the work while that person is gone*

*The work waits until the employee returns*

Regardless of which of these two things happen it is clear that there has been no additional cost incurred by the organization for this paid time off. Since the person is on salary the yearly cost of that person's pay and benefits is fixed regardless of the number of days or hours that they actually work in any given year.

**With this in mind, why wouldn't a company use extra vacation as the flag that they fly for their salaried employees? Even farther down this path is the idea that instead of a pay raise each year why couldn't we**

**allow the employee choose between additional pay and additional time off during the year?**

Now clearly there is a limit as to the number of vacation days that an employee can have during the year and still be able to effectively serve the company...but what is that number? My thought is that our goal would be to get every salaried employee to the point of 3 or 4 weeks' vacation VERY early in their career with your company.

This would serve as a barrier to entry for competing companies and a hard thing to give up for your current employees in order to take a job somewhere else.

I'm not sure exactly what the right number of weeks vacation is appropriate for your company; you can figure that out for yourself. What I do know is that the coming generations of workers are very likely to continue valuing flexibility and time off more than anything else in choosing an employer. Why not be known as the most flexible employer with the most vacation in your industry? The alternative is to try and be the highest paying employer in the industry...and that is a tough battle to win. If people will come to you for money they will also leave you for money.

Try to rethink your ideas about time off with these new ideas in mind and you can find yourself as the employer of choice in your industry. It is fruitless to try and impose your standards of what was important to you in your career on this new generation of worker. The trend is undeniable and will continue as far as the eye can see.

## CHAPTER 5

# Change what you are interviewing for

I'm known for having some ideas about hiring that go against almost everything that we THINK we know about. It is incumbent on any organization to change their hiring strategy when things are not working well for them. If your current recruiting and hiring methods are not working for you it is important to change something. Or as Dr. Phil might say:

*"How is that workin' for ya?"*

I'd like to turn our attention now to the way you ultimately choose new employees through your interview process. If you are not getting the right people into your organization there are only two possibilities:

*The right people are not applying for the jobs or*

*You are screening out candidates that could do a great job for you in your hiring process*

If very few people are applying for your positions then it is clear that either your message is not compelling or you are not putting it in a place where people looking for work can easily find it.

If you get lots of applicants but the people that you end up hiring turn out not being great fits for your organization then it is incumbent on you to change your resume screening and interview process. I mean, what are the chances that you had 50 applicants for a position and ALL of them are UNABLE to do a good job for you? Maybe you are just asking the wrong questions...

I'd like for you to consider a couple of concepts that may change the way you look at and evaluate candidates entirely:

- People get hired for what they know (experience and education) but they almost always get fired for how they act (who they are as a person).

- Whoever you hire into your organization and regardless of how much education or experience they might have, you are going to spend the first 6 months of their career with you teaching them your companies' way of doing everything.

Let's take a look at each of these and discuss how they might impact and possibly even change the way you recruit and evaluate candidates.

### People get hired for what they know (experience and education) but they almost always get fired for how they act (who they are as a person).

Why do we spend so much time in the hiring process on evaluating people based on their experience? If you really think about this it has been done this way long before we had all of the tools we have today to evaluate the whole person as a candidate for our company. Long before there was LinkedIn, the only way to separate the "wheat from the chaff" for incoming resumes was to see if the person had a specific set of skills and experience. There was no other option. My belief is that this process is used today simply because it was created 100 years ago and each generation was trained by the last.

### But what if there was another way?

I'd like you to think for a moment about the best people that work for your organization. The ones that you rely on, brag about and count on every day. Is it really their technical skills that make them so valuable? The fact that they always deliver, are never late, solve problems before they get to you, are great leaders and your customers love them usually has nothing to do with their technical skills...do they?

Now there are jobs that require a certain level of education and experience for sure. If I'm having open heart surgery I want someone who has done it 100 times before and was educated at the finest medical college in the country. If someone is designing the safety of the car that my family drives in you better bet that their knowledge of engineering safety into a car matters. So I'm clearly not talking about every job here. Although, you will often have several candidates that all have roughly the same education and experience...so how do I decide?

Next I'd like you to think of the last two people that you had to fire from your organization. Not lay off due to slow sales but fired them for cause. What did they do that got them fired? Did those actions have anything to do with their technical skills or education? Likely not. More than likely they got fired because of their interaction with other people (peers or customers). Or maybe because they lacked the drive to get things done on time. Or perhaps they lacked accuracy in their work just because they lacked focus or dedication to the task. When you examine the people that you fire one strange realization will likely come to you:

**We hire people for what they KNOW (experience and education) but we fire them for WHO THEY ARE (the way they treat other people).**

Take a second to think about that. If you hire a person who does not have the exact right experience or education but they are fantastic people and work endlessly to get things done, how bad can it be? How much damage could they really do? How would others in your organization react to their hiring? My guess is that if they were great people, others in the organization would be more than happy to give them whatever training or help they needed to be successful.

Now imagine the other extreme. Let's say that you hire someone that is incredibly qualified with education and experience...but they always rub people the wrong way. They gossip and create trouble. They lack responsibility.

How much damage can they do to your organization? A LOT!

No matter how qualified someone is their success as an employee is going to be almost solely based on how other employees and customers react to them. Even the greatest technician will fail if they consistently anger or disappoint those around them. So why in the world don't we screen people for those abilities at least as much as we screen for technical skills? Mostly because it takes time and effort...it is less efficient...but can be much more effective. And with the advent of LinkedIn it is pretty easy to do.

### *Stop asking for resumes and have people apply only using their LinkedIn profile.*

LinkedIn is what I refer to as a "3 dimensional resume". As opposed to a flat sheet of white paper with black ink on it that we call a resume, LinkedIn allows so much more information to go on in the hiring process. Their profile allows you to look at recommendations from others. It shows you who you are connected to that is also connected to the candidate so you can message them for a reference.

The employee can demonstrate skills sets and show examples of their work. They can post articles that they have written or news reports of achievements. You can get a much better idea of the whole person you are considering.

### *Why would anyone NOT use LinkedIn for people to apply to their company?*

The answer sadly is the same as it usually is: "We've always done it this way." A poor excuse for not using one of the biggest advances in job search and candidate screening that has ever occurred. Does it take some small changes to your process? Yes. Does it take a little more time to review the candidates file? Maybe. But what is the cost of getting a hire wrong? If you had the opportunity to know more about candidates before you evaluated them why wouldn't you?

Lastly, it also solves another age old problem of interviewing: not being able to confirm statements made by the candidate. Most candidates are honest and tell the truth. Some do not. LinkedIn has the potential to allow you to talk to other people that have worked with this person in the past and confirm their story. What is the saying? Trust but verify. This is especially important if you are interviewing for a leadership role in your organization

**Whoever you hire into your organization and regardless of how much education or experience they might have, you are going to spend the first 6 months of their career with you teaching them your companies' way of doing everything.**

You have a training program for new employees right? You have a mentor program that allows them to shadow an established employee to see how things work right? You have processes and procedures for doing virtually everything that your organization does right? You have quality control provisions to make sure that every product or service that leaves your organization meets with strict standards right? You have a supervisor to "show them the ropes" and guide them along the way right?

*If all of that is true why does a person's education or experience even matter?*

Again, for highly technical jobs like engineering and medical pursuits experience is crucial. But I'm guessing that most of the people that you are hiring into your organization (especially for entry level opportunities) do not fit into those categories. Maybe an accountant fits into this category, but a sales person certainly doesn't. Your customer service people can have literally no experience with your products and services and still be amazing at their job. Remember, you are going to train them to do so.

I believe that the intense focus on education and experience is only an exercise used to efficiently screen 300 resumes into a manageable number of candidates (like 30 or so). If you want to continue to use that for the initial screening process fine. But what in the world are you doing using it to make final decisions between two equally qualified candidates?

My belief is that once the initial screening is done education and experience should be almost completely disregarded for the rest of the hiring process. This would require the screening person in HR to only forward to the interviewing committee those candidates that they know could be successful in the chosen job if the applicant's information is accurate. From that moment on education and experience should play no role in the decision making process. If each of them are qualified for the job then the only evaluation from this point on should be on how they fit in the organization and whether they have the drive and desire to do the job.

Are you struggling with this? Good. Take some time here to convince yourself that I'm wrong. Evaluate all of the truly great people in your organization and then determine if their technical skills and experience is what makes them great. Convince yourself that that the last person that you fired was worth keeping around (even though they created chaos) because their technical skill added so much value. See. You already know this is true but you are likely just struggling with the logistics of changing your hiring process to make this change. You might be concerned that this change will be too expensive or complex for your organization to adapt. The good news here is that if you are WILLING to try an experiment, I can make your organization ABLE to do so.

In a 2014 survey, thousands of HR managers were surveyed across the country and asked which "soft skills" were most important to a new employee's success.

**Their answers were:**
*Communication*
*Creativity*
*Initiative*
*Problem solving*
*Teamwork/Leadership*

As you look at this list I'm going to ask you to once again picture in your mind your most valued employees. Do they shine in one or two of these areas? As I mention each one of these traits does the employee in your organization who is best at it jump into your mind? I'm guessing the answer is yes. What we know for sure based on experience is that if an employee comes to work each day and excels at these 5 things they will be wildly successful.

Now look at the list again and think of the last two people that you fired. Can you identify which of these traits they violated on a regular basis? Do you immediately recall your frustration with them as you tried to get that struggling employee to be more effective at one or more of them? Can you remember the act that they did that convinced you that it was time to let them go?

One more time I'm going to ask you this question:

**When was the last time that you fired an employee because they were physically or mentally UNABLE to do the job? (Crickets chirping)**

So if your best employees are the best not based on technical skill and experience, and the people that you end up firing are not let go because of a lack of technical skills or experience then what in the world are we doing using those criteria for anything other than the initial screening of applicants?

I would be hard pressed to tell you the number of job seekers that have come back to me and told me that the company hired someone else with more industry experience. It would be in the hundreds for sure. As I talk with them I always wonder why the hiring committee defaulted to that excuse for making their choice. My guess is that the hiring manager creates a more defensible position for themselves if the new hire turns out to be the wrong hire. Can't you just hear the conversation?

"Well I'm really sorry that Janet didn't work out. I was very sure to hire the candidate with the most education and industry experience. How could I possibly have known that she would be rude to customers and disruptive with her coworkers? You can't really know that from a resume or a one hour interview. I guess she fooled all of us...but I did MY part."

You can see why your employees might want to default to that as the final decision making piece for two candidates that are pretty equally qualified. You can also see now why it is the worst possible way to make that decision. If candidates do not have the initial education or experience they should never make it through the initial screening process. If they do make it through that process then the only reasonable criteria to make your final decision on is their ability to demonstrate the 5 soft skills listed above in their past work.

This is where the change to using LinkedIn for people to apply to your jobs really comes into play. This tool allows them to have others vouch for their ability in all 5 of these soft skill areas. You can ask permission to connect with them (from the candidate) and then communicate with someone who has worked with them in the past.

You can review examples of their work and see their endorsements. Then you can contact those people (again with the candidate's permission) and ask them why they endorsed them for that skill. The possibilities of confirming that a candidate is who they say they are almost endless. Far, far, far superior than you could ever get with any form of resume.

---

## How to interview for soft skills

Behavioral based interviewing is used in many organizations across the country. The problem is that there is no way to confirm that the stories that the candidate is telling are true. I'd like to think that all candidates will be honest but the fact is that the allure of a new job can get the better of a few of them. Candidates rarely out and out lie but have been known to stretch the truth some. The secret to this type of interviewing is to change the questions surrounding these soft skills in a way that will not allow candidates to prepare for them.

Most candidates have a good feel for behavioral based interviewing. There are a hundred websites that show them the questions and the right way to answer each question. Given the ability to anticipate the questions even the least qualified job seeker can create convincing stories to show their worth. To get the truth it is important to throw them a curveball.

What I have learned after doing more than 1,000 interviews in my career is that surprise is the only way to get a genuine response from a candidate. The good ones prepare for what they think might be coming. Here is my idea to get a real answer from them:

Instead of asking them to tell you about a time that they did each of the soft skills well, ask them to tell you a story about when they FAILED to use that soft skill well and how did they recover from it.

This small change will be quite unexpected for the interviewee. It is in no way a trick question as it simply asks about a time when they didn't use the skill well. It is not something most people will prepare for.... And that's why it will produce a truthful and thoughtful answer.

Genuine people are as WILLING to talk about their failures and what they learned from them as they are their successes. It is part of the learning that makes them who they are. They are generally not ashamed of the learning...they see it as a natural way to find out what works and doesn't work. We learn almost everything in our lives through a process of trial and error. How could this be any different?

A genuine and humble person may blush a little in telling the story because they are not proud of what they did. But all any of us care about in this case is "What did you learn from it?" This allows them to tell you how they recovered from it which is equally important to doing it right.

In my experience the egotistical or non-genuine person will try to talk around their mistake or even make it the other person's fault. The "clever" person who is trying to be someone that they are not will shift the blame to someone else or try to minimize the impact of the error. These are exactly the kinds of people you want to keep OUT of your organization.

What I know after all of this time is that if an organization knows who someone actually is then they will have a great deal of success teaching and developing them. If we know an employee's true motivation we can adjust our messaging to them in order to help align with the values of the organization. As long as we hire employees that are actually trying to improve as people and employees then we stand a fighting chance of helping any struggling employee get back on a path that will serve both them and the organization.

The employee that is trying to hide something or trying to portray themselves as something other than they really are is an employee to avoid at all costs. How do I know that? It is really a combination of two things:

Having managed hundreds of employees I have seen this to be true

### I USED TO BE ONE OF THOSE EMPLOYEES

While I am not proud of this I will tell you that in the mid 1980's I was a young and pretty clueless young man. I had dazzled people for so long that I actually thought that I had everyone fooled. Several times in my very early career I found that I could pretend to be someone I wasn't and get just about any job that I wanted. For low level jobs this was a fine formula for advancement...as long as I was WILLING to sell my integrity for money. Then I met Bill.

Bill was the HR manager of the paper mill that I had worked at for about 5 years. I was an hourly employee that literally started there sweeping the floor. While I had moved up to higher level jobs over the years I now wanted to be considered for a salaried supervisor position. I had no idea what a revelation I was in for.

During the interview process I used all of my best prepared lines. How I was "very interested in the company succeeding and in the welfare of the employees that I would be managing". How I would always be faithful to my manager but would never do anything that I thought was not the right thing to do. In my mind I was putting on a masterful performance...and then the walls fell in. The seasoned HR manager who had seen it all sat back in his chair and just stared at me for a moment- he then unleashed a tidal wave of honesty that forever changed the course of my career. To the best of my memory he said something like this:

*"Mr. Czarnik, are you telling us your true thoughts or are you telling us what you THINK we want to hear? You may think that you have everyone in this room fooled but let me tell you what I see. I see a young man who will say anything to get this next job not because he really wants the role but because it will put him in the spotlight and in a higher position with some small amount of authority. I see someone who is so full of baloney that it is hard to tell where the baloney ends and the real Chris Czarnik begins. I think you have no business at this time being a supervisor. If you are going to continue to talk and act this way I suggest you leave here and become a used car salesman. We do not hire people who are WILLING to stretch the truth to get whatever suits them. You are not ready for an opportunity like this. I suggest that you go back to work and decide who you want the world to see you as. You are a smart guy Chris...maybe just a little too smart for your own good."*

Leaving that meeting was perhaps the lowest I had ever felt at any job. He was not mad or purposely hurtful. He simply gave me the professional dressing down that I so richly deserved. For the first time ever I think I realized that I wasn't fooling anyone and worse yet, everyone around me saw me for what I really was. A smug, self-important and egotistical person who would do or say virtually anything to get what he wanted.

Someone to whom the truth was simply a suggestion. Someone who would lie straight to the face of others about my intentions and my expertise to get a job I thought I deserved. I did not deserve the supervisor position. At that moment I thought that I deserved no position at that company at all. It was one of the seminal moments of my career and believe it or not I am forever thankful for the favor that Bill did for me that day. I needed a swift kick in the pants...and he happily obliged.

Here's the point. In my opinion the main purpose of any interview is to determine two things...and ONLY two things:

*Does this person really want this position and is it a good fit for both them and the organization?*

*Can you believe the words they are saying?*

If you think about all of the employees that you have struggled with and eventually had to let go I would challenge you to come up with one that didn't fit into one of these categories. Remember:

"After we hire any new employee we are going to spend the next six months training them to do everything our way anyway. The only things that really matter with any hire (after the initial resume screening to find qualifications that fit) are whether the person fits and how customers and coworkers will react to them on their first day."

How does your interview process stack up against those criteria?

## CHAPTER 6

# Engage and Retain the great talent you worked so hard to get

As I mentioned in the outset of this book there are really three different parts to winning the war for talent. The first is recruiting great talent, second is engaging and retaining great talent, and the last is developing talent to be your next generation of leaders. Let's talk for a second now about engaging and retaining the employees that you've worked so hard to get.

It's kind of amazing to me that employers are so incredibly focused on the front end of the employment life span. Most organizations who are struggling with not having enough talent OR enough employees in their organization seem entirely focused on how to bring new talent into the organization. That is of course necessary but what they miss is that as they are bringing three new people in the front door because two of their existing employees are walking out the back door to go work somewhere else. It's a little bit like trying to fill a bucket with a hose and not fixing the hole in the bottom of the bucket first.

It's important for you to understand the reasons that people leave organizations... And they're not that complicated. Studies have been done on this topic and the results are very consistent. There are 3 main reasons why people leave organizations and we'd like to deal with each one of them now:

*The employee is in a job that does not come naturally to them or is inappropriate for this skill set.*

*Negative interactions with their direct manager or supervisor.*

*A growing opinion that they are being taken for granted and they do not see a pathway to growth for themselves either personally or professionally in the organization.*

Let's take time here to dissect two of them and talk about the problem and what you can do inside your organization to plug the hole in the bottom of the bucket. We'll discuss the third one in the next chapter

## The employee is in the wrong job

It has become incredibly clear to me that putting an employee in a job that is not appropriate for their skill set or their personality is a ticking time bomb. Many of you reading this book right now have been in jobs in the past that you struggled with every day because you didn't enjoy it or it just didn't fit. An employee will put up with this for some period of time. As soon as they believe that there is no progression and that this job (the job that is so difficult and frustrating for them) is their job for the long-term they will almost immediately start looking for another place to work. There is perhaps nothing more frustrating to an employee then doing a poor job even though they are doing the very best that they can. In other words a main reason that people leave organizations is that companies put square pegs in round holes.

The loss of an existing employee because they are in a job not appropriate for their skills, abilities or personality type is very expensive. Consider for a moment that most studies suggest that the cost of replacing an employee in an organization is 50% of their annual salary. That means that replacing a $50,000 employee is approximately $25,000 in time, effort, training and lost productivity. I say this very specifically for those managers who do not want to spend money on training for engaging their employees. If we assigned a cost to every employee that left our organization we would quickly see that any money spent on training and engagement pays for itself very quickly. Unfortunately most organizations are only focused on cost on the front end and once they have the employee in place they no longer track or even consider the cost of that employee leaving. That was mostly the case because there were always other employees that could be hired. That is no longer true today.

I would ask you to consider something that we have discussed previously in the book. If your employee is doing an average or below-average job in their job there really only two possibilities. They are either UNWILLING or  UNABLE to do the job with a higher degree of proficiency.

And as we talked about earlier it is very rare that any employee purposely does a poor job. That means that an employee that is doing a substandard job anywhere in the organization is most likely a victim of poor training or of being in a job they never should have been in the first place.

What decades of personality profiling has taught us is that each personality type of the 16 total personality types has a set of skills, abilities and jobs that they will naturally do very well. It also means that jobs or responsibilities that are outside the natural fit of people with a certain personality type will cause havoc with their happiness and your organization's productivity. Adding this type of evaluation to your hiring process does not have to be difficult or expensive at all. In fact many of the very high-functioning organizations have applicants for any job, internal or external, take a personality profile before they are even allowed to apply. If the personality type that comes out from their test is not one of the personality types that is a natural fit for the type of job you're interviewing for, that person is immediately eliminated from consideration. While that might sound harsh to you think of the amount of time effort and stress that you as a manager have spent with employees who you could easily see were in the wrong job.

Of the dozen or so people that I have had to fire in my life at least 10 of them were in the wrong job. What is even more fascinating is that for many of them after they were let go they told me later that being let go from that job made their lives much better and removed stress from their lives. Considering that personality profiling has more than 80 years of experience over tens of millions of people there's probably something to it. For each of the thousands of people that I work with individually, the very first thing that I do is have them take a personality profile. We then take a look at their personality type in terms of whether the job they just left was a natural fit for them. Almost without fail those people were square pegs in a round hole. Being let go had nothing to do with being bad employees. It had everything to do with the fact that no matter how hard they tried the task they were asked to do was simply not something that came naturally to them. So they failed on a daily basis.

The main cause of this "square peg in a round hole" problem is hiring just anyone under time constraints to fill the spot. There's an old saying that I have become incredibly fond of in the hiring process and that saying is this:

*"If you need it bad, you'll get it bad."*

I hope the meaning of this phrase is not lost on you. Most hiring is done under a time constraint. Most organizations only hire when things get so bad that there is no other option. They are in such a difficult situation that they have to hire whoever they can as quickly as possible. There never seems to be enough time to do a thorough evaluation of the employee on the way in the door especially when it comes to finding if their personality fits both the organization and the job. The problem is that if you need somebody in the job bad, you will likely get somebody in the job bad. Then you will spend the next several months or years fighting to make somebody fit into a position that they never should have been considered for in the first place. Their technical skills are fine but they just don't belong doing that kind of work.

## The Solution

The interesting thing here is that if you would like to make this happen inside your organization you can make it happen for exactly $0. That's correct you can implement a strategy to increase the effectiveness and appropriateness of every hire for no cost other than a little bit of time. How can you do that? The answer is in the website www.16personalities.com. This website contains a free personality test and results for every personality type once it is determined. Included in that is a list of jobs that is appropriate for each of the 16 different personality types. While the exact job they are interviewing for might not be on that list, jobs with similar duties and responsibilities could be a great fit.

There is obviously much more work to do here and I have helped many organizations across the country implement this kind of strategy. The first step however is likely for you to take this test and prove this idea to yourself. You will be stunned at the results of implementing this kind of idea on the front end of your hiring process. While personality testing is not perfect, for 80 years and over tens of millions of people it has been a reliable indicator of how people act, make their decisions and interact with people. Maybe it's something to pay attention to.

## Negative interactions with their direct manager or supervisor

Study after study suggests that the number one reason people leave a job is negative interactions with their direct manager or supervisor. In fact this is so prevalent that we will spend time here talking about not how to change your employees but how to change your managers and supervisors into people that your employees really want to work for. Think about the last job you left. Was it really about money? Was it really about the type of work that you were doing? Or was it more likely the fact that your daily interaction with your manager or supervisor did not give you hope that things were ever going to get better... or that they actually valued you as an employee? If you're honest with yourself you can probably identify the best and the worst manager that you've ever had in your career. Interestingly enough it's probably difficult for you to remember the really positive things about the best boss you ever had. You may remember in general terms some of the sentiments that made them good but the actual day-to-day interactions are hard to focus on. It's hard to put your finger on exactly what they did right every day in order to become such a great boss.

The opposite is true with the bad bosses in your life. My guess is that you have very clear visions and pictures in your mind of the manager treating you badly. You very likely can identify the moment that you knew that you had to leave this organization because this manager was going to make every day a living hell. Or maybe the manager wasn't actively evil but simply didn't pay attention, wasn't interested in you or your growth and took you for granted.

My guess is that you can easily point to the moment where you said enough is enough I'm not taking this anymore!

The solution is relatively straightforward but it comes in two different forms. As we talked about in the paragraph above, personality profiling is a great way to determine whether somebody can be an effective leader. The mistake that many organizations make is that they take the most senior person in any technical skill and make them the manager of people. Then somehow the organization is surprised that this person (that was an amazing technical person) ends up being really bad with people and they get complaints about that technical person's leadership style.

*It's as if you found the most reliable car in the world and then decided to use it to cross the ocean.*

This type of promoting people goes on in the vast majority of organizations. The assumption of course is that if somebody is good at the work then they will be good teaching other people to do the work. While that would make somebody an outstanding technical trainer it is zero indicator of how well they will be able to lead and train people and turn them into an effective team.

Think once again about the best managers that you've ever had. Do you remember them as being the most technically capable person in the organization? Not likely. More likely is the idea that that person was compassionate, a good listener, fair and had the ability to motivate people to work effectively in a team. How am I doing so far?

## The Solution

If your organization is not actively putting your managers and supervisors through leadership training consider starting that immediately. There are dozens of programs out there and many of them are very good. It would be inappropriate for me to call any one of them out because I've not had the opportunity to evaluate all of them. But suffice it to say that you are not the first organization that is looking for leadership training for your managers. There is however one facet of leadership training that you can start tomorrow and can do for almost no cost.

Many organizations have brought me in to teach leadership inside the organization. The place that I always start is teaching active listening. What is active listening? Well, the fact that you don't automatically know shows you how little effort we have put into making people good listeners. Organizations value people who can speak well. Many of the most highly paid people in your organization are likely in those roles because they can inspire people, help customers in a time of need or close the sale. As a society we value extroverted speakers as they symbolize strength confidence and intelligence... at least that's what we think. The problem is that most managers that are struggling with their employees are first and foremost struggling with listening. Here's a question for both that speaks to this:

*"When was the last time that an argument you had was not a misunderstanding?"*

Maybe take a second here and relive the last argument that you had with your significant other. This argument could have been about anything. Maybe it was about taking out the garbage, paying bills, raising children or housework. Think for a second about how that argument unfolded. There really only two possibilities in any argument. The person was either UNWILLING to do what you asked or they were UNABLE to do what you asked. Now try and think about the last time anybody didn't do something that you asked simply because they were trying to make you mad. Or they didn't do what you asked them to do because they were just trying to stick it to you. Almost never. The fact is virtually every argument starts as a misunderstanding...and the basis for almost every misunderstanding is an inability or unwillingness to effectively listen. My suggestion here is that if you fix the listening part of communication you will not have to spend any time at all on the talking part.

What is active listening? Well again, I'm not going to suggest any one particular program because there are many outstanding programs out there. But I can give you an idea of the basics of active listening. While it may seem like more work initially if we spend a little more time up front to understand each other and where we're coming from, we don't have to spend all the time on the back end unraveling the anger and frustration of the misunderstanding.

Active listening is teaching people that listening is much more than simply waiting to talk. Active listening is all about not only hearing the words, but understanding the **_intent_** of the person that you're listening to. This is most easily achieved by repeating back to the person speaking to you a summary of what they just said **and** what you believe their intentions were. It's not just a misunderstanding of words that gets people in trouble... It's a misunderstanding of the intentions behind those words.

Think about email for a moment. I would describe email as a communication tool as very efficient but not very effective. Don't you remember the last time you got an email and were very confused at what you believed the message was? Without any verbal cues like volume or intonation all you had to go on were the words that actually showed up on the screen. It was very easy to misunderstand the intentions of those words. After you had a chance to talk with the person who sent you the message the words made perfect sense. Once they explained the background of the statement and what they hoped to accomplish, what they said quickly came into focus. The trouble is that in between the time of reading the email and actually getting the explanation of what the email was supposed to say there is a moment of misunderstanding and potential for frustration and anger. Active listening is an attempt to take away this possibility.

For the purposes of this book I am not going to try and teach you active listening in this text. That's the great thing about the internet. Virtually everything you need you can find with a few short keystrokes into Google. More importantly, if you're asking to implement this as a solution there are many models online for zero cost that you can implement. Often I am brought into an organization to teach active listening and it's the first thing that we do in trying to solve significant disagreements. Heck, maybe the first step for you is to try at home.

My strong belief is that if you begin to model active listening at the highest levels of the organization it will quickly filter down to every level of the organization. Taking time out of the work day to actively teach this to your employees is an indication to them that they are really important and that any misunderstanding between them and their manager can be managed and can be fixed. Perhaps most importantly it is up to your managers and supervisors to understand that it is their responsibility to initiate fixing problems of misunderstanding. That only they have the authority to take the actions to take the fear and anger out of most manager/employee relationships. That most employees will stay silent for months and perhaps even years before they approach their manager with the issue. So it is up to the supervisor or the manager to identify indicators in a person's work that may be one of the first signs of frustration in the relationship.

There are two indicators that are good telltale signs of trouble between an employee and a manager. The first is absenteeism and the second is substandard work. Let's just take a moment and cover each one of them and discuss why it's so important to track these indicators inside your organization.

## Absenteeism

One of the easiest patterns to spot in an employee's work life is their attendance. Identifying problems of any sort in an employee's work or home life usually plays out with difficulty coming to work. Frequent attendance issues are a reliable predictor of trouble in any relationship with an employee. The trouble is that most organizations deal with attendance issues in an entirely negative way. It would be common for the organization to call the employee in and make them aware that their attendance is becoming an issue. The organization will most likely site chapter and verse from the employee manual that talks about the consequences of not being to work on time or taking an excessive number of days off of work. At best this method will scare the employee into compliance...if that's your goal knock yourself out. But I'd like you to think about the last time you were going through a significant issue in your home or work life. Was your attendance affected? When you were dealing with marital issues or financial issues or overwhelming stress didn't you have occasion to either come to work late or leave work early more often than normal? If it was true for you my guess is it's true for your employees as well.

If instead of tracking attendance issues for the intent of implementing progressive discipline we look at it as an opportunity to check in with the employee to find out what's going on and how the organization might be of help. We will win over the employee's heart and their mind. While many organizations have EAP (Employee Assistance Programs) programs that allow employees to get help with home or life situations we rely on the employee to start that conversation. What if we used attendance issues as a way to show that we care? What if we called people in not to scold them but to check in with them to see what's going on in their lives. What if we used the opportunity of abnormal attendance to show the organization that we care about them and their life both at work and away from work? Using it in this way might be new thinking but it also is the way to engage employees during emotional times and build an emotional bank account with them.

Attendance issues are usually a cry for help. You can either take that cry for help and punish it for reaching out or you can reach out and see how the organization can be of help. If you want your employees to be loyal to you it starts with you being compassionate with them.

## Substandard work

Another relatively clear indicator of difficulty either with a manager - or something else going on in their life - is an employee beginning to turn in substandard work. This might include not getting enough work done, the work having mistakes or being inaccurate. Either way an employee that has typically turned in excellent work at the correct and required volume and

## Everybody Wants to Build Their Own Path

The third reason employees leave is that they lack vision for how they will develop in the organization and a lack of understanding about what control they have over their future. This happens more often than you would think. Most organizations spend a great deal of time on the front end of hiring people in, making sure that they get the very best people that they can. They take time to train the person and make sure initially that they are doing a really good job and are happy. But after several years it is common for an employee to become frustrated and even disgruntled with the lack of development inside the organization. This frustration is a growing seed of angst that eventually blossoms into looking for a new job. The problem is this frustration normally goes unnoticed or unseen by the employee's direct manager until the day that employee gives their notice. And when that happens it is very common for the manager to say to that employee "Why didn't you tell me you were unhappy?"

The better question is, why wasn't there a plan in place for the employee to guide their own career and keep themselves satisfied and challenged throughout their entire career?

At a base level I'd like to make this observation: It seems ridiculous to me that anyone should have their development in the hands of someone else. The only reasonable expectation is that employees be given the opportunity and the tools to be in charge of their own career and their own development. This is the basis for all of the work I do in the Internal Career Mapping (ICM) area.

Think for a moment about the last conversation that you had with your direct supervisor in your annual or semiannual review. My guess is there was some long conversation about what went on during the year, what things went well, and what the expectations were for accomplishments going forward. These were pretty straightforward conversations because we were talking about things that had actually occurred or were well defined future goals. This part of a review is generally done pretty well in organizations. It is the last part of the review process that most managers and most organizations struggle with. That part we call the development plan.

Do you remember your last conversation about a development plan for you? My guess is there were some vague generalities discussed around communication or cross training or increased responsibilities within the organization. It all sounded great to you. The problem was there was nothing concrete to execute that plan. In fact, your manager was responsible for your career path in terms of showing you opportunities to grow personally and professionally. I don't know about you, but the only person that I want responsible for my future... is me. But is that really possible? The answer is yes... but only if organizations are both WILLING and ABLE to give the control of their future to the employee to manage.

My belief is that most employees would gladly take responsibility for their own development inside their organization if they were given the chance. More importantly, the feeling of being in control of their own future is the glue that will make employees want to create a 5 or 10 or even 20-year careers with a single organization. If you are reading this, my guess is this seems pretty attractive but might seem out of reach.

The promise here goes far beyond getting employees to stay in your organization and saving the cost of turnover. The real opportunity by implementing development planning (driven by the employee themselves) is to create succession planning that can be guided, monitored, encouraged and measured. The equation here is relatively simple. The employees want control over their career. The management of an organization wants to develop the next generation of leaders. Why not give employees the tools and the systems to conduct their own internal career mapping as a research project that they are responsible for?

## What is Internal Career Mapping?

I have been teaching proactive job search for almost two decades. The vast majority of my clients have been midcareer or late career professionals. My task with each one of them was to teach them to do a research project so that they could identify and seek out their next employment opportunity. They did so by systematically learning to understand their personality type, their achievements and skills, a vision for the next job that they would be searching for and then to gather information from people who live in the world they want to live in next. To learn and confirm that this type of opportunity was an appropriate next step for them.

If people can be taught to do a job search outside of their organization, doesn't it make sense that we could teach them how to do a job search inside their current organization and create a plan and a pathway to their next promotion? As importantly, with the employee driving their own search, the responsibility and work to create and execute this development plan could create almost no additional work for the employee's manager or their human resources department. While this may sound far-fetched to you initially, you will come to see that it is actually the only method that is logical, sequential, auditable and predictable. Most importantly, the feeling of being in control of their own future is the glue that keeps people in the same organization for decades. While most employees currently have to rely on hope for their next promotion, your employees can set their own course, do their own research, prove to the organization that the job they have targeted is a great fit and conduct all of the internal research to confirm their hypothesis.

The benefit of this type of program inside your organization that you may not have thought of or considered is its ability to create employee initiated crossfunctional and cross departmental conversations inside your organization. This can lead to increased communication and decreased confusion and misunderstanding. My guess is that if you could encourage these types of conversations within your organization that would be a pretty positive thing for you. The beauty here is that these conversations are a natural end result of the internal career mapping conversations that employees will be having every day. So how exactly does internal career mapping work?

What do employees lack currently that keeps them from being able to identify future opportunities inside your organization?

My guess is it boils down to three things:

1. *Knowledge of what their personality type and* transferable *skills sets are and what problems they solve*

2. *A systematic way to sort through positions in the organization that are a next logical fit based on their education, experience and desired career path*

3. *Access to information about those positions from people who have or have had those jobs in the past.*

All we require as an organization to encourage and empower employees to create their own internal career map is to make them ABLE to perform that research project inside their current organization.

---

## How Internal Career Mapping works

The process that I am suggesting has been proven effective by me with more than 2,000 mid-career professionals. More importantly is the realization that the process that we're about to discuss has been used by companies to develop and sell every type of product ever sold. That's correct. I teach people to identify and find their next opportunity the same way that Campbell's sells tomato soup. The same way that Hershey sells you a Mounds bar. The same way that Porsche sells expensive sports cars to 50 year old men. This process is not only proven over the last decade by me but influences you every single day in your own life to get you to purchase items both large and small. This is not a theory. In fact, this is very likely the way your marketing department has chosen to sell your products or services to your customers. I trust that you will find it most familiar.

The process that I have taught them has three basic steps:

**Definition, Research and Confirmation (Marketing)**

I'd like to discuss each of the steps with you so that you can fully understand how this process might work inside your organization.

---

## Definition

Definition is the process of figuring out what something is and what something is not. What it does, and what it does not do. Where it has value and what problems it solves. Considering that the work around definition is going to be based on the employee themselves I'm not sure we could find a topic that could interest your employees more. What we know for sure is that everyone's favorite topic is themselves. If we base a new program inside your organization and the first step is for people to be able to learn and talk about themselves you won't have a lot of difficulty selling the idea.

2000 years ago a philosopher named Aristotle had chiseled into a stone arch the saying: "First Know Thyself." Another phrase that many of us have heard is that "the unexamined life is not worth living". Both of these sayings mean that there is nothing more interesting to any human being than learning more about who they are and why they do what they do. In this process of definition the employee will not only learn about themselves at work, but as importantly how they function and make their decisions outside of work and in their personal relationships. Every new program implemented in an organization needs a hook. A reason that employees will see it as more than just the program of the week. A reason that employees will not only start the process but work diligently in order to continue their progress day in and day out. My work has proven that there is nothing more motivating to a human being than the promise of learning about why they do what they do.

In the definition phase this employee is going to learn everything they possibly can about their own personality type through online research. This will help them better understand their values, how they make their decisions and what is truly important to them.

The next step is for your employees to write out five of their most significant work-related achievements. They should write them out in paragraph form. The purpose of this exercise is to not only identify when the employee was doing the correct work in the correct situation but to identify their natural skills sets.

Now take a look at each of those achievements. Identify which of those skills were most commonly associated with their achievements. In this case each employee will identify the skills that they are most comfortable with, enjoy doing, and as importantly have used to create an outstanding end result.

The last step in the definition process is for the employee to create a hypothesis based on what they have learned from their achievements and skills about the type of work, the type of responsibilities, and the types of problems they hope to solve in their next position. This hypothesis might look something like this:

*A position involving* _____,
_____ *and* _____
*for a* _____ *department focused on*
_____.

It might sound something like this: "I am looking for a position involving monitoring safety, quality and productivity for a manufacturing department focused on continuous improvement and lean manufacturing ideas."

The reason this step is so important is that it is very common for an employee to simply say "I'm looking for a job with more responsibility or in a different department". With this type of vague generality it is impossible for them to identify actual positions that exist inside an organization that they would like to focus their research on. The ability to clearly define the tasks, duties responsibilities, level and deliverables that they hope for in their next position is a critical piece for them to be able to examine all positions that exist inside their organization and find those that fit.

Having this hypothesis completed before they ever begin the research phase is absolutely critical. There is an old saying that "if you don't know where you're going any road will get you there". That is very true in internal career mapping. The thing that holds employees back from being able to identify and develop into the next level is a lack of knowledge of themselves, their skills, and the types of problems they are already good at solving.

---

## Research

The research phase in internal career mapping begins with using the skills that the employee identified during their definition phase. The goal here is to use those skills and those terms to search through a list of job titles and job descriptions inside the organization using a keyword search so that only jobs that fit those criteria are shown as possibilities to the employee. That may not seem like a difficult task if your organization only has 10 different job descriptions. But consider an organization that has more than 20,000 employees more than 50 different locations and almost a hundred different job descriptions. Without this process how could an employee have any possibility of knowing what jobs inside the organization potentially could fit for them? In fact, I would suggest that the number one reason that employees do not currently drive their own development inside an organization is because they just don't know what possibilities exist.

Consider for a moment that the only time that most employees review any type of job title or job profile is when the job is actually open. Really, when else do employees have the opportunity or the occasion to review the job descriptions inside the organization? The trouble is that when the job is actually open it is far too late for employees to start this process in order to determine whether the job that is open is actually a good fit for them. That process of Internal Career Mapping must happen long before any job becomes open and long before they are eligible to apply for it. There are a couple of reasons for this:

*The first reason is that without the ability to know themselves and their skills how could any employee identify the kind of work that they want to do going forward?*

The second reason is that an employee's willingness to actively work towards a job inside the organization before the job is actually available is the best indicator possible of that employee's true interest in that position. It is this willingness to identify and commit to developing the skills needed before it opens that ensures that the employee not only knows what they're getting into but also has the skills to successfully perform the job.

Another part of the research phase of the process involves the employee not only identifying a position that they believe is a natural fit for them going forward, but the need for them to justify their decision and prove their hypothesis with facts and evidence with their own manager or somebody in the Human Resources area. To be clear, this process has nothing to do with people getting whatever they want inside an organization. That's just Madness.

What this process does allow is for the employee to come up with an idea and to try and sell the idea to either their manager, their Human Resources staff or someone else in the organization that confirms that they're heading in the right direction. The side benefit of these conversations of course is that the employee will be actively engaged in conversations with their manager more often and the conversations will be positive and about themselves. The conversations will be the employee showing pride in the research that they've done and convincing their manager or somebody else in authority that the target job that they have identified makes sense.

It is only after this hypothesis is confirmed with somebody in authority that the employee is given the go-ahead to conduct the last phase of this research project which we were referred to as Confirmation.

---

## Confirmation

After the research phase of the process is complete the final phase is called confirmation. The long and short of confirmation is that up until now everything the employee knows or thinks they know about this position is conjecture. It is based on what the employee thinks that they know about what it takes to be successful in this next job. Confirmation is exactly what it sounds like. Confirming by talking with people who do or have done the job that this position is what they thought it was and that they still want to continue their development path towards filling that role.

There is little worse in an organization than having the wrong person in a role. In the confirmation phase the employee will conduct informational interviews with people inside the organization who have direct knowledge of the duties, responsibilities and requirements to be successful in the targeted roll. There is no replacement for learning about a roll or talking to people who have been in the trenches and successfully executed the roles requirements.

As with the other parts of the process the confirmation phase runs through the employees' manager or a trained coach. During the employees' conversation with their manager they will ask for advice as to which people inside the organization the manager believes would be helpful to talk with about this position. During this conversation the manager and the employee will again confirm the goals and the reasons why this particular position inside the organization has been set as a future goal. This additional conversation between the manager and the employee can do nothing but strengthen that relationship.

After the manager suggests a person inside the organization that the employee should talk with the employee sets up a conversation with that person who has experience that they can learn from. They can get that person's view on the role and the appropriateness of the role for the employee going forward. The employee will ask for that person's advice, guidance, and feedback as it applies to their research project regarding this potential future opportunity. The employee to this conversation will learn all of the pluses and minuses, responsibilities and deliverables of the role. Through these conversations the employee will make a final determination about if this role is a great fit for them going forward. They then set this role as their new target development opportunity.

## The Gap Analysis...the Final Piece in Employee Driven Development

With all of the research completed the last part of Internal Career Mapping has to do with creating and executing what I refer to as a Gap Analysis. It is the closing of these gaps in order to make the employee fully qualified for the target position that is the real payoff for this process.

In order for an employee to be fully qualified for the position that they have targeted for their next internal opportunity, there is very likely going to be both educational and experience gaps that exist. With their manager or their internal coach the employee identifies what experiences and what education they would need to be a serious candidate for this position the next time it becomes available. With this knowledge the employee can execute a self-determined plan to not only develop themselves and their skills but be a serious candidate for higher level positions inside the organization in the future.

The last step in this entire internal process is to watch employees to see if they actually work on filling the gaps that they identified in their Gap Analysis. This will include sharing with employees what resources are available from the organization that might help them fill those gaps. Those might include educational reimbursement, job shadowing or internal training programs that are designed to improve the employee skill set. In this way it becomes clear to the employee that the organization is genuinely interested in their development and wants them to make it to their next level inside the company.

There is another side benefit. Most employees will take advantage of this opportunity and actively work to fill the gaps that they identified during the process. Some employees will not. For those who choose not to actively engage it is an indicator to the organization of that employee's willingness to engage in their own development and advancement. Unfortunately, some employees will say that they will do anything to move up in the organization but when the opportunity comes there is always an excuse or reason why they do not do the work. Internal Career Mapping will allow any organization to quickly identify whether an employee is truly interested in moving up in the organization not based on what they say... but based on what they do.

With this idea in mind I would suggest that most employees do not develop inside an organization not because they are UNWILLING but because they are currently UNABLE. They lack a clear executable process in order to drive their future success in the organization. There is nothing more motivating in the world for any employee than self-interest. A company's future success relies on its ability not to plan an employee's future for them, but to give them the tools to create that pathway for themselves.

This is the promise of winning the war for talent. No program of the week. No fairy dust and no quick fix. You will win the war simply because you will find, engage and develop the best talent possible. Isn't that all anybody is looking for?

# Postlude

## Becoming an Employer of Choice

Eight years ago in the midst of the Great Recession few companies were focused on becoming an "employer of choice." An Employer of Choice means that with all things being equal (pay, benefits, vacation, etc.) people will choose your organization to work for over your competitors. In that time period most organizations were just worried about weathering the storm and keeping their doors open. It is in this period of time that Employers of Choice step to the forefront.

When organization say that "our employees are our greatest asset" I always wonder if that is true in tough economic times. When employers ask me "where has the loyalty of employees gone?" I want to ask them how many people they laid off during tough times. There is an old saying: "I don't believe anything you say....I believe everything that you do." Loyalty for the most part has become a one way street. An employee is expected to give two weeks' notice but when the company fires them or lays them off their employment is terminated immediately. Employees are asked to pitch in when the company is struggling but few companies reward their employees beyond their salary when very profitable times return.

With an idea of leveling the playing field in mind let's take a look at a couple of very actionable things companies can do to improve their organization and its relationship with its employees:

## 1. Focus on Hires of Opportunity

What is a hire of opportunity? Well, to put it simply it is hiring a new employee that you come across because they are such a perfect fit for your organization... even though you do not have an open spot for them at the moment.

If you are a football fan, just think in terms of the annual NFL draft. When coaches and general managers are asked who they have targeted to select to join their team their response often sounds something like this:

*"We are going to draft the best player available regardless of position"*

What they are saying is that regardless of the short term needs of the organization they will draft a great player even if they do not have a specific need at that position. The idea here is that the goal is to fill the organization with great people and great athletes and that will raise the overall talent of the team. Think of the saying, "A rising tide raises all ships."

During the course of running your business you are going to come across truly gifted and talented people looking for work. Many will say: "If I only had a job for them I'd hire them tomorrow." The idea of hires of opportunity means hire them today and find a place to use their talents. The only problem with hiring people only when you need them is that your search for talent will be rushed and only include who happens to be in front of you at the moment. *Remember, "If you need it bad...you'll get it bad."* Hiring when the pressure is on limits your options and can make you commit to substandard candidates. If you find great talent today... hire them today.

I can guess what some of you are thinking: "We can't afford to carry extra people!" My thought here is that you limit hires of opportunity to about 3% of your workforce each year. Aren't you going to lose 3% of your current workers sometime this year? How about we find their replacements when we find great talent... not under the gun of a person suddenly quitting.

## 2. Look for great talent in your everyday life

There is the charismatic leader of a group of car dealerships that employs around 1,500 people. He is committed to filling his organization with great people and teaching them everything they need to know about the car business (aren't you going to do that with every new hire anyway regardless of their background?) I got to witness this first hand.

In the college Employment Connections office that I managed I had an amazing intern.... let's just refer to her as Jordy. Jordy was a ray of sunshine every day that she came to work. Our staff loved her, our students loved her and she had an amazing "find a way to say yes" attitude for every task that was requested of her. I was bound and determined to help her find a great job after she graduated.

One day Jordy came in and screamed out, "I got a job...and it's awesome!" How had she gotten this great opportunity? Hundreds of resumes and interviews? Nope. She had been working her way through college as a barista at Starbucks. Every morning this leader came in for coffee he was greeted by Jordy's wide grin and happy voice. This went on for more than a year. As graduation loomed he asked Jordy to give him a call. He hired her within a couple of weeks. No car experience and very limited administrative experience. No matter. What he wanted was that smile and can do attitude in his organization....he just happened to find his next great personal assistant at the counter at Starbucks.

### 3. Conduct exit interviews, but only with great employees who leave for a great opportunity

I am a big fan of exit interviews. These are the interviews that the company conducts with people leaving the organization so the organization can get their thoughts about their time working there. The trouble is that many organizations hold these mostly with people who they fire or layoff. What do you think you are going to get from those people?

There is a real opportunity though holding an exit interview with great employees that leave your organization for the most positive of reasons...they got a great promotion that was not available to them in your organization. It is here that valuable information about what is going on inside the organization can be learned. I would suggest that you hold these exit interviews a couple of weeks after your employee is in their new job with the other company. Why? Leaving a company is an emotional time. Strong loyalties are still at play and it may affect the employees WILLINGNESS to be fully transparent.

Doing the exit interview after the employee has been in their new company a couple of weeks gives them an opportunity to compare and contrast the two places of work. They also are far enough away from the emotions and loyalties that may have affected their message. Maybe offer them a $50 gift card for a nice dinner if they are WILLING to participate. The rarest quantity for any leader is the unabashed truth. That opportunity lies in this moment.

---

## 4. Create talent pipelines within your associations ... or even with competitors.

I'm guessing I'm getting a few strange looks with this one. Work with my competitors? Yes...work with your competitors. I know that for certain levels of talent in an organization you may be in direct competition for employees with your competitors. But as we move up the ladder to leadership positions, opportunities for your great people may just not be available in the foreseeable future.  Face it, if there is no advancement opportunity for them in your organization eventually they are leaving one way or another.

Being in touch with other organizations in your industry allows each company to find talent that already has technical knowledge. As new leadership opportunities come up the HR people or CEOs of those companies can share leadership roles they are looking to fill with others in the industry. If you have a great employee that is frozen or stuck, making them aware of other opportunities will buy you loyalty for all of the remaining employees. The message will be clear...we want you to succeed. We'd love for it to be here but we will not hold you back.

If you are discrediting this idea as you read this, just remember one thing: *Great employees that cannot develop with you are leaving anyway.* Don't tell your employees you care about their growth...show them.

## 5. Make educational reimbursement available to all employees and encourage it by making it easy to access on their schedule.

Generally people want to grow. As someone who was managing in the Technical College system for almost 10 years I can tell you that most people are WILLING to learn and improve. Most don't because they believe that they are UNABLE. Not having transportation. Not having the money. Not being able to fit into the schedule of a class.

All of these are reasons that I have been given a hundred times over from students saying that they couldn't go back to school. Maybe 20 years ago that was true... not today. If you contact your local college or technical college you will find learning opportunities that you had never imagined. Blended courses, fully online courses, courses that run on demand. Your old ideas of needing to let the employee leave work on the clock to go to school is outdated. The world of education has spent the last 5 years becoming more flexible and more accessible than ever before.

While I think this is a great way to invest in your employees, I believe two things about providing this:

> *The employee needs to do the training on their own time...not the company's time. The rules are different if people are going through a trade internship or something like that but for the most part you want the employee to have some "skin in the game".*

*Ask the employee to pay for some percentage of the cost of the class-maybe 20%. Anything that is easily gotten is not much valued. Again- don't tell me you want additional training...show me.*

Before you walk away from this one I would encourage you to check in with your local colleges, technical colleges and trade schools. You might be very surprised at the possibilities they can provide.

## 6. Don't get stingy with medical or bereavement leave.

Think about the state of mind that an employee has when someone they love is in the hospital or has just died. More than just being UNABLE to focus, their every waking second is preoccupied with what they are going through...as it should be. How long they have to handle this event should not be one of their concerns.

Maya Angelou famously said, "No one will ever remember what you did, no one will remember what you said...but NOBODY WILL EVER FORGET THE WAY YOU MADE THEM FEEL". Everything you do during this emotional time that they are going through will be deeply cemented into this employee's memory...good or bad. This is one of the rare moments where you can win the employee's loyalty with an indelible memory. Don't waste that opportunity.

I am not suggesting that you have unlimited paid leave for these event. There must be a limit so the company can run. But why not give one more day of bereavement leave than anyone else. You will never remember that day...they will never forget it. Additionally offer as much unpaid time off as they choose to take. This is where they can show you how important this event is to them as well. These events happen infrequently but create lasting impressions. What side of history do you want to be on?

## 7. Don't answer What...Answer Why

In all of my years doing this type of work, the most common reason for someone to leave an organization was disconnection from the organization. The employee believed that they had become a replaceable cog in the machine. They did their task, got paid and went home. I work today, you pay me today and that is the extent of our relationship. Remember, your employees can get that anywhere.

No matter what job I have had in my life (sweeping the floor, running a machine, managing a process or managing people) I had a need to understand WHY I was doing something. There was a great deal of training about HOW to do each task. Not telling the person why can often make an employee feel as if they might not understand these higher level concepts. That can come across as very insulting. How do we expect any employee to develop in our organization if they are not WILLING or encouraged to ask why? Higher level jobs in any organization are simply people who have a broader and deeper understanding of WHY things are done the way they are.

If you want people to remain with you it is important to show them daily that you trust them and that you want them to grow. Explaining every new task with not only the WHAT but also the WHY feeds a person's natural need to grow. And maybe, just maybe helping them to understand WHY will bring about ideas that you had never considered.

# Want to be an employer of choice?

*Show people on a daily basis that given the choice you will always choose people over profit.*

*If you do so, you will likely never have to make that choice again.*

# Author Bio

Chris Czarnik has spent 20 years analyzing hiring from every angle. He has served in HR, Hiring manager and Operations manager roles for Fortune 500 companies for more than a decade. Chris knows the joys and frustrations of trying to find people that truly fit an organizations culture and values.

From the other side of the desk he has provided outplacement services to more than 2,000 mid-career professionals. This experience has given him a perspective few have. Chris not only understands what employers are looking for, but also understands why people come to and leave organizations...and what they are truly looking for from their next employer.

In 2013 he created the Human Search Engine process that serves job seekers. This process is used by colleges and organizations across the country... including in the US Congress. Internal Career Mapping was the next logical step after all of the work he has done inside organizations over the past decade.

Chris owns Career [RE]Search Group with his wife Jennifer Banta-Kroll. Together they create digital and print products to help people find the right role in the right organizations, and organizations find the right talent for their culture.

# Resources

**You can learn more about us, our company and our products (or follow our blog) at:**

www.careerresearchgroup.com

**Find us on LinkedIn at:**

https://www.linkedin.com/company/career-research-group/

**And connect with us at:**

https://www.linkedin.com/in/chrisczarnik/
https://www.linkedin.com/in/jenniferbantakroll/
https://www.facebook.com/MyHumanSearchEngine/